AQUA

21 JANUARY –

CW00446511

Russell Grant's

1990 HOROSCOPE

A STAR BOOK
published by
the Paperback Division of
W. H. Allen & Co. Plc

CONTENTS

INTRODUCTION

Welcome to my new astrological guide to begin the decade ahead!

If you start the day wondering 'What is in store for me?', then my 1990 forecasts are written especially for you! Once you've chosen the book written for your zodiac sign, then you can enter the decade ahead with complete confidence, knowing that I've outlined all the astrological trends that the planets have lined up for you. Even though these stars are general for your sun sign (you'll need an astrologer to give you a personal forecast based on the time and date of your birth), I still take astronomical information to produce the astrological interpretation.

Having pin-pointed all the possible potentials, as well as the pitfalls, for the coming annum (and I outline all your love, cash and work prospects in a special section), now all you've got to do is tune in on the starry trends surrounding you and turn them to your advantage! Easy, isn't it! Remember that forewarned is forearmed and whilst there's nothing totally fatalistic about Western astrology, it can indicate all the benevolent, benign and bothersome beams that will be coming your way. Act accordingly and you'll be able to achieve your ambitions, realise your heart's desire and begin to develop your true potential. Good luck!

Do you read my stars column and wish that you knew a wee bit more about the planets and what they mean? Then turn to the first half of this book and read my guide to the ten planets that

1

make up our astrological agenda. Knowing more about your own planetary ruler will teach you something about yourself and the way you relate to the world around you. And if you're a regular reader of mine, you'll know how important the Moon is in astrology. Understanding more about Moonpower will give you insight into the moods, emotions and feelings of folk around you.

With the help of my section on Venus you'll be able to discover for yourself exactly how the movements of this loving planet affects you during her zodiacal cycle. If you've ever wondered how or why you attract certain people, where you'll meet the love of your life or who turns *you* on, then this could be when you listen to the beat of Venus's heart and find out all you've ever wanted to know about *amour*!

Relationships are all about communicating with the folk around us, and we all know how much easier one-to-one affairs can be with the help of a little understanding and appreciation of each other. Well, in this book you'll find my descriptions of the twelve signs of the zodiac, giving you an intriguing insight into everyone you know. As well as that, there's also a section telling how your sun sign gets on with the rest of the celestial set-up, who complements who and an instant guide to sun sign compatibility – you could be in for a few surprises! And last but not least, if you've always wanted to discover your lucky number or most favourable colour, then turn to the astrological traditions and you'll discover everything you need to know.

I hope that this book will help you make 1990 and the start of your decade, an era of success, satisfaction, sunshine and smiles all round. Happy reading and happy days!

Russell

RUSSELL'S GUIDE TO THE PLANETS

What is astrology? Those of you who regularly read my columns, books or magazines or watch me on television will know that the science of astrology extends far beyond the zodiac and the different characteristics of each of the twelve Sun signs. In fact, that's just the tip of the iceberg, because it's the movements, behaviour and actions of the ten planets in our Solar System, as seen from the Earth, that are really what astrology is all about. The planets travel around the Sun at varying speeds and distances.

The zodiac is divided into twelve segments, each 30° wide, ruled by the twelve Sun signs. However, each of those signs is governed by one or two planets, as you can see from the chart, and it's the relationship that these planets bore to each other at the time of your birth that influences your personality, and gives an astrologer a unique insight into your character. They can modify, accentuate or conflict with the effect that the Sun has on you, and a completely accurate horoscope is a map of the heavens charted for the exact moment that you were born. It's like a blueprint of your character, with all your potentials, pitfalls and problems there for the discerning astrologer to divine. If you've ever had your horoscope cast, then you'll know that it makes fascinating reading.

Each planet controls a particular aspect of your personality, whether it's your innate emotions, the way you respond to your mother, or your sexual drive, as you'll see from the descriptions on the following pages.

RUSSELL'S GUIDE TO THE PLANETS

SIGN	SYMBOL	RULER	ELEMENT	QUALITY
Aries	Ram	Mars	Fire	Cardinal
Taurus	Bull	Venus	Earth	Fixed
Gemini	Twins	Mercury	Air	Mutable
Cancer	Crab	Moon	Water	Cardinal
Leo	Lion	Sun	Fire	Fixed
Virgo	Virgin	Mercury	Earth	Mutable
Libra	Balance	Venus	Air	Cardinal
Scorpio	Scorpion	Mars Pluto	Water	Fixed
Sagittarius	Archer	Jupiter	Fire	Mutable
Capricorn	Goat	Saturn	Earth	Cardinal
Aquarius	Water Carrier	Saturn Uranus	Air	Fixed
Pisces	Fish	Jupiter Neptune	Water	Mutable

THE PLANETS AND THEIR INFLUENCES

THE SUN

The ruler of the Solar System, this is the body around which all the other planets revolve. Just as we on Earth would die without its life-giving rays, so a horoscope is centred upon the Sun, and the placing of the Sun in someone's chart indicates their ego, individuality and behaviour patterns. It also shows their potentials, drives, creative urges and abilities, so it is always a very important factor in someone's horoscope.

Positive traits of the Sun include *joie de vivre*, artistry, open affection and a love of children. On the other hand, negative characteristics include pomposity, arrogance and a very overbearing nature. Each planet rules a different part of the human body, and the Sun has power over the heart and spine.

The Earth takes a year to complete one orbit of the Sun, during which time the Sun passes through each of the signs in turn. The position of the Sun in its particular sign and house of your horoscope will show the way in which you express yourself. The Sun rules Leo, the most regal sign of all.

THE MOON

After the Sun, the Moon is the most important planet in an individual's horoscope, for La Luna governs emotional responses, the unconscious side of the personality and the links with the past. What's more, she influences our maternal instincts as well as our desire for emotional security.

As well as ruling the tides and even the actions of many shellfish, the Moon is also associated with motherhood. After all, she affects the female menstrual cycle, the nervous system and is also believed to control some people's sanity – hence the word lunatic. The Moon plays such an important role in our day-to-day lives that I have devoted a whole chapter to describing her effects as she traverses through each of the twelve signs during her monthly voyage through the zodiac.

The positive characteristics of the Moon include a good memory, maternal feelings, sympathy, empathy and a passive nature, but negatively she can mean someone who is moody, tenacious, unreliable and easily swayed by their surroundings. The Moon rules Cancer, the sign of the Crab.

MERCURY

The nearest planet to the Sun, Mercury is never more than 28° away from that heavenly body, and is known as an 'inferior' planet. In a birthchart, Mercury may appear in the same sign as the individual's Sun, the preceding sign or the following one. Mercury is the planet of the mind, signifying the drive within us all to learn, gather knowledge and also to communicate it to others. Amongst the positive Mercurial traits are good communicative abilities, perception, cleverness, versatility and a gift for concentrating on details. The other side of the coin is a love of malicious gossip, extreme nervous energy, inconsistency, a hypercritical character and a sarcastic tongue.

Mercury controls two signs, Gemini of the Air element and Virgo of the Earth element. In the human body, Mercury is associated with the respiratory system, the brain and the thyroid gland.

VENUS

Like Mercury, Venus follows the Sun's orbit through the heavens, and is never placed more than 48° from it. She is the second of the 'inferior' planets. So, in a horoscope Venus is either in the same sign as the Sun, or found within two signs to either side of it. Also known as the morning star, Venus is recognised as the planet of beauty, harmony and the ability to love.

Not surprisingly, she is considered to be a very feminine influence in someone's horoscope, and the house in which she falls indicates the individual's capacity for love and harmonious relationships. People with a strong Venus in their charts can be extremely attractive or even beautiful, as well as being gentle, kind, refined, placid and understanding, with a strong need to be surrounded by lovely things. However, negative Venusian traits include laziness, a weak will, an excessive love of romance and a very sugary or even gushing manner. Venus governs the Air sign of Libra and the Earth sign of Taurus, both of which are renowned for their fair faces and love of beauty.

As far as the body is concerned, Venus influences the throat, kidneys and the lower back. Many people with a strong Venus in their horoscopes have beautiful singing or speaking voices.

MARS

Although smaller in size than the Earth, Mars exerts a considerable influence over us astrologically. It represents our energy, aggression, sexual drive and therefore the masculine instinct in both the sexes.

6

Mars is known as a 'superior' planet, because its orbit isn't influenced by that of the Sun, so in a horoscope it can be found in any of the Sun signs. It takes approximately two and a half years to complete its journey through all the twelve signs, and on average stays in each sign for just over two months. Amongst the positive Martian characteristics are abundant energy, dynamism, pioneering instinct and a lively nature, whilst the negative traits include aggression, selfishness, brutality, rudeness and a hasty approach to life. The two signs controlled by Mars are Fiery Aries and Watery Scorpio, which is also influenced by Pluto.

In the human body, Mars rules the red blood corpuscles, cuts and burns, muscles and the adrenal glands.

JUPITER

Gigantic Jupiter is the largest of all the planets, so it's not surprising that it rules expansion, whether physically or mentally. Its orbit is rather erratic, and it spends much longer in some signs than in others, but it takes approximately twelve years to complete one cycle through the zodiac.

Jupiter has a very strong influence on our outlook on life, and is associated with optimism, good luck, opportunities, success and happiness, as well as religion, the search for knowledge, politics and philosophy. People with a strong Jupiterian placing in their birth charts can be entrepreneurs, have a very positive approach to life, are jovial, loyal, benevolent and with good intellectual powers. Negative traits include undue optimism, never knowing when to say no, extremist beliefs, conceit and a self-indulgent streak. Jupiter rules the Fire sign of Sagittarius and shares the rulership of Watery Pisces with Neptune.

The liver, pituitary gland and thighs are all influenced by Jupiter.

SATURN

The rings that surround Saturn speak volumes about its characteristics, for it represents restrictions and limitations. The influence it exerts in a birth chart is a very serious and sober one, pin-pointing an individual's inhibitions and secret fears, so to an astrologer Saturn's position in a horoscope is a vital indication of someone's character.

Although traditionally Saturn is regarded as very dour and stern, it is also an extremely constructive and crystallising force, helping us to realise our goals through self-discipline, wisdom and determination. The two signs ruled by Saturn are Earthy Capricorn and Airy Aquarius, which is also influenced by Uranus.

Amongst the positive Saturnian characteristics are practicality, patience and pragmatism, a sense of responsibility, duty and diligence, loyalty and conservatism. Negatively, the traits include out-and-out pessimism, depression, dogmatism, cruelty, aloofness, an inferiority complex and parsimony.

Slow-moving Saturn takes approximately two and a half years to pass through each sign, therefore completing its orbit of the Sun every thirty years or so. Saturn is associated with the teeth, bones, skin, rheumatism and the gall bladder.

URANUS

The first of the three 'modern' planets, Uranus was discovered by William Herschel in 1781. Far larger than the Earth, Uranus lies a very great distance from the Sun and takes about eighty-four years to complete one journey through all twelve signs of the zodiac. That means it spends approximately seven years in each Sun sign in turn, and so is seen as a generational influence as well as a personal one.

Traditionally associated with unruly change and revolution, Uranus controls all the modern sciences, from television and computers to space travel and anything else that's futuristic. It is also the ruler of Airy Aquarius, the most forward-thinking and unconventional of the twelve signs. The positive Uranian attributes include humanitarianism, a love of freedom, originality, inventiveness and a visionary sense. Perversity, rebelliousness, anarchy, eccentricity, intransigence and wilfulness are some of the negative effects.

In the human body, Uranus has influence over the nervous system, the circulation of the blood, paralysis and sexual perversions.

NEPTUNE

Nebulous Neptune is the second of the three 'modern' planets, having been discovered in 1846. Even larger than Uranus, Neptune's distance from the Sun means that it spends about fourteen years in each Sun sign, and therefore takes about 168 years to travel through the complete zodiac.

Like Uranus, it exudes a generational influence as well as one that is more personal, and is known as the higher octave of Venus. As a result, Neptune is associated with very spiritual, supernatural, aesthetic, artistic and refined subjects, and is the joint ruler, with Jupiter, of Watery Pisces, which is the most sensitive and ethereal of the twelve Sun signs. As its glyph would suggest, Neptune influences all maritime matters, but also hospitals, prisons and similar institutions, since it creates a social obligation that must be fulfilled. In fact, Neptune rules the saint as well as the sinner – not only the person striving to help those in need, but also the one who is needy.

The key word for Neptune is illusion, so it's no surprise that it rules the cinema, poetry, dancing, gases and drugs. Positive Neptunian traits include idealism, imagination, creativity, nostalgia and sensitivity, but the other side of the coin is escapism, deception, diffusion, distortion, undue worrying, corruption and chicanery. Like a magician, Neptune can delight or deceive you.

The spinal column, mental processes and nervous system are all influenced by Neptune.

PLUTO

The newcomer to astrology, Pluto was discovered in 1930, making it the third and last of the 'modern' planets. The most distant planet of all, Pluto has a very eccentric orbit and can stay in some signs for as much as thirty years, whilst it travels through other signs in a far shorter time. In all, Pluto takes 248 years to complete a single orbit around the Sun.

Because of the cataclysmic and catalytic events taking place when Pluto first came to light, it is associated with elimination, transition, transformation, regeneration and rebirth. It can be destruction and death or the aspiration to higher things. As well as its effect on a generation, it also has a strong influence on individuals.

Pluto, along with Mars, rules Watery Scorpio, the enigmatic sign associated with change, metamorphosis and evolution. Positive Plutonian aspects include the ability to start again or rise like a phoenix from the ashes of a previous path through life, the gift of analysis and investigation, and a capacity for dealing in big business. Conversely, Plutonian traits can be cruelty, self-destruction, compulsion, jealousy, criminality or sadism.

Physically, Pluto rules the reproductive system and the regenerative forces of the human body.

RUSSELL'S GUIDE TO THE SUN SIGNS

ARIES – 21 MARCH–20 APRIL

Talk about tireless! Just watching some of these aerated and aerodynamic Arians arabesquing about, full of the joys of spring and with big grins on their faces, is enough to make several other signs want to lie down in darkened rooms, or reach for the aspirin, until they're sure the show's over and it's safe to come out again. After all, folk who belong to this sign are imbued with energy, enthusiasm and enough get-up-and-go to send them hurtling through life at a very hectic pace indeed!

Arians belong to the first of the twelve signs of the zodiac, which makes them the babes of this celestial wood. And because they hail from the sign of the Ram, they can be very bright and bubbly baa-lambs indeed. In fact, there are three sorts of Arians: those racy, rough-and-tumble Rams who are quite likely to knock you over with their effervescent energy (talk about snap, crackle and pop!); the less loud, laughing Lambs, who'll ask you to come out to play; and the slightly silly Sheep, who always follow the rest of the flock.

As if that weren't enough, Aries is also the first of the three Fire signs, making them hot-headed and hasty-tempered to a dramatic degree. Although they can be inflamed with enchanting ebullience, they can also be devoured by a rampant rage and fly off the handle in the twinkling of an eye. The trouble is that they're overflowing with fearless, Fiery energy which has to be released in positive, controlled

10

ways. Arians belong to an astonishingly active, athletic and sporty sign, so whenever they're frustrated, fed up or full of fervent feelings fizzing away inside them, they should rush out into the open air and do something strenuous!

Arians are ardently ambitious, assertive and aggressive, and they know exactly what they want out of life, as well as how they're going to get it. That's because they're one of the four Cardinal signs, and also because Aries is the sign of the self. 'Me' is their favourite word. (No wonder that one is their lucky number!) Somehow they just can't help putting themselves first and everyone else second – a trait that makes them seem selfish and self-obsessed sometimes, when they disregard or completely ignore the feelings of others. What's more, they can be so sure of themselves that they can turn into bullying bossy-boots, issuing commands, instructions and orders left, right and centre. That's because they can never forget their desire to be first in everything they do, and at times it can push them right over the top in trying to get their own way.

Martial Mars is their planetary ruler, and no one messes about with him in a hurry! (Well, in Roman mythology he was the god of war, which should give you a jolly good idea of what he was like.) A lot of Arians have red hair, but even if they've got black barnets or not a single strand left on their heads (and lots of Arian chaps go bald at a very early age), they'll still have a fantastically fiery temperament, so watch out! Most of the time this Martian mélange are very light-hearted and cheerful, but once they lose their rags they can really let rip. Shouting, screaming, ranting, rampaging and creating a furious furore are all ways in which this boisterous bunch let off steam, but luckily their tantrums and tirades are usually over as soon as they've begun. They'll feel much better for getting it off their chests, though everyone else will be quaking in their boots and wondering what's going to happen next! Even so, their tempers may get really out of hand and become violent in extreme circumstances. There's no doubt that these are the folk who get so irate and irascible that they could murder someone in the heat of the moment. If you know an Arian who easily flies off the handle, then make sure they get lots of physical exercise 'cos that's the best way in which they can work off their wrath.

One of the things that gets these rapacious Rams hopping mad is being told what to do. Unless they want to be thrown out on their ears for ignoring the boss's instructions (they'll do it their way or not at all!), they should go for a career in which they can call the shots. Something sporty, the Army or even working with cars. (Arians love driving full speed ahead.) When it comes to hatching brainwaves, ideas and showing their intelligence, these ardent Arians have definitely got it made. The trouble is that they aren't exactly suffused with sturdy staying power once they get bogged down with boredom, and could easily fritter away their enormous potential by abandoning a pastime or project halfway through or handing it over to someone else to finish off whilst they seek out the next exciting enterprise. Just by increasing their perseverance and dogged determination, ambitious Arians could soon find themselves sitting on the top rung of the ladder of success.

Martian maids and men are pulsating with the spirit of adventure, and there's nowt they like better than setting off on their hols for somewhere new and exciting. (There's no going back year after year to the same old places for this pioneering pack.) If they can't afford to trek off to explore the jungles of Africa just like Tarzan (that's right, he's a raring-to-go Ram as well!), they should still try to take off for pastures new as often as possible.

Now, the interesting thing about all these Arians is that underneath that fluffy, funny, exuberant exterior lurks a huge heart that can be very easily hurt indeed. You see, for all their bravado and bravura, it's in all the amorous areas that Arians come a cropper most often. They can skip along, gathering strings of admirers and having a whale of a time, but the minute they meet a mate who makes their heartstrings ping and bluebirds start singing in their ears, they'll forget about all their other sweethearts and turn fantastically faithful. When they're in the mood, they're real romantics – and when they're in another sort of mood they're right old ravers, wanting a very erotic emotional encounter indeed.

TAURUS – 21 APRIL–21 MAY

Gigantic chocolate cakes, mighty meat puds, lashings of gorgeous gravy and the sort of grub that mum used to make – they're all the Taurean's idea of heaven. Mountains of fabulous food come very high indeed on their lists of priorities, and when they haven't been fed and watered to their heart's content they can produce some very rancorous roars.

There's something soothingly solid (must be all that food!), safe and serene about this lot, and they make other folk feel that they're deliciously dependable. Because they're stolidly straightforward and utterly uncomplicated, you always know where you are with a terrific and trustworthy Taurean. Unless, that is, they have some more complicated planets in their birth chart, in which case they'll take a bit more working out and understanding.

These fundamental folk belong to the sign of the Bull, and you only need picture one of these bovine beasts to understand those truly Taurean traits. Most Bulls like taking life easy, and it's leisure and pleasure that make them tick, 'cos they crave and cherish their creature comforts. Just think of a beautiful bull or a carefree cow munching its way through a meadow and you'll see the Taurean idea of the ideal existence. And this second sign of the zodiac is ruled by voluptuous Venus, who gives Bulls a tremendous taste for the good life. This pretty planet also endows many Taureans with luscious looks and velvety voices, though she may help them to put on the pounds as well if they've got a very sweet tooth or the sort of hearty appetite that makes Henry VIII look like a modest eater. Even if the avoirdupois advances at an alarming rate this lucky lot will still manage to turn more than their fair share of heads whenever they trot around town.

'Down-to-earth' is one way to describe this bovine bunch, and that's quite a coincidence when you consider that Taurus is the first of the Earth signs. Not surprisingly, these Bulls need to be near nature if they're to feel fully at peace with the world, whether they're in their own back yards or standing in the middle of nowhere, hearing the bees buzzing and the birds trilling away. Lovely! In fact, whenever a Taurean is feeling down in the dumps or as though life just ain't worth living, they'll soon perk up if they can get down to doing some gardening.

If you want to give a Taurean the collywobbles (but you wouldn't, would you?), the merest mention of change in their lives will make them turn pale and reach for the whisky. Alterations are anathema to these steadfast folk, and they like to know in advance what next month is going to bring, let alone tomorrow. Trying to persuade them to have their holiday in a new county or country could be your life's work (they've probably been going to the same old place for years), and they can get all hot and bothered at the thought of having to change their routine. That's because they come from the Fixed element of the astrological set-up, though stubborn, intransigent or obstinate as a mule can be other ways of describing it! Let's face it, once their delightful determination gets out of hand, and they're sure they're right and you're wrong, they can dig their heels in and refuse to budge one inch.

Never mind, because the 'F' in Fixity also stands for faithful, and this loyal and loving lot will stick surely by their sweethearts come what may. In fact, they're so loyal, true and trustworthy that they're quite content to have one partner for the whole of their lives, no matter how many ups and downs they meet along the way. All the same, that can cause problems for these doting Bulls in the sentimental stakes if they've fallen for someone who's an out-and-out rat and doesn't deserve the devotion, or if love fades and dies between them and their other half. They'll still want to stay by the side of their partner even if they know deep down that they'd be better off apart, and they may put up with almost any amount of unhappiness rather than call it a day.

Quality not quantity is the Taurean motto when it comes to choosing chums, but the few friends they do have will be mates for life. (And if you're one of this happy breed let's hope you know how lucky you are!) When it comes to entertaining, Bulls are in a class of their own. They make smashing hosts and hostesses, and are happy to throw open their doors to their nearest and dearest, give them a warm welcome, fill them full of food and get them laughing with their terrific Taurean sense of humour. No wonder folk beat a path to their doors!

As you can see, stability is something Bulls search for, and they don't ever feel really safe and secure until they're surrounded by signs of their own wealth or worth (or both – some of this sign can be real moneybags!). Everyone needs a roof over their heads but ideally Taureans need to know it's theirs, and not just rented from someone else. Putting their hard-earned loot into bricks and mortar is one of the best ways for a Bull to blow their boodle, and they'll love living in what's also an investment for the future. They're not mean or miserly, but they do like to make their money work for them! Possessions are of paramount importance to our Bully buddies, and they'll work all hours of the day and night if they've got the prospect of a bulging pay packet at the end of it.

Farming, gardening, cooking, banking, real estate and anything artistic are all perfect professions for boy and girl Bulls. When they're at work, Taureans plod steadily on and will prefer to be one of the backup team rather than stars in their own right. (They're much too modest and unassuming to stand in the spotlight, unless some more show-loving signs are prominent in their birth charts.) They believe in doing things slowly but surely, and though they may drive some fast and furious folk into a frenzy of frustration with their careful and considered ways, they know that they'll get there in the end. A round of applause please for these tremendous, terrific and tender Taureans!

GEMINI – 22 MAY–21 JUNE

Charming, captivating, engaging, entertaining, gregarious and – Gemini! You can never know too many of the folk belonging to this sign, though if you've got a nervous nature you could find their lively, loquacious and lightning fast ways too much to cope with.

Communication is the name of the Gemini game, because they're ruled by that mischievous midget, Mercury. In Roman mythology, mini Mercury was the messenger of the gods, dashing hither and thither like a demented dervish, and Geminis can be just the same. Most of these folk could keep the Post Office and British Telecom going single-handed, as they need to be in touch with pals, partners and anyone else who takes their fancy. There's nowt they like better than a chinwag with their chums on any subject under the sun (they'll yak away about anything from crochet to croquet, carpentry to chemistry), a dynamic discussion about the state of the world that lasts for hours on end or running up a phenomenal phone bill. Go shopping or out on the town with one of this sociable bunch and they're bound to run into lots of people they know. Making friends and influencing folk is as easy as falling off a log for such chatty types as these.

Another name for mercury is quicksilver, and that describes the Gemini personality to a T. You'll either love it or loathe it, but these folk can change their characters in the twinkling of an eye. It's all because they're one of the four Mutable signs in the zodiac, making them very adaptable, changeable and mobile. One minute they can feel gloomy and glum, and the next they'll be scintillating, sunny and acting as though they hadn't a care in the world. If you're rather set in your ways you could find their chameleon quality hard to cope with, but maybe you ought to spare a thought for them and wonder how they feel about it!

Not for nothing is this said to be the sign of the Twins, and many folk born when the Sun was in Gemini have at least two people inside them jostling for position. Now, don't start muttering words like schizoph-renic, or Jekyll and Hyde, under your breath, for it simply means that these twinkling Twins can always see at least two sides to every story, and may feel merry and miserable, careless and cautious, responsible or rebellious, all at the same time. Makes you feel confused just thinking about it!

Talking of thinking, that's something Geminis do a lot of, thanks to their Airy element, which makes them very intelligent imps indeed. Like their fellow Air signs of Libra and Aquarius, they've no time for dolts or dullards because they prefer the company of people who've got lots of brainpower and aren't afraid of using it. Life's bound to be far too short for these curious creatures, because there's so much they want to learn about the world, and so little time to do it in. Have a look at the older Geminis you know and you'll notice that they're still young at heart. These are the folk who'll take up hang-gliding when they're ninety, learn Latvian at eighty or put their young friends to shame by knowing more about the pop scene than they do!

There's only one problem, and that's that the Mercurial attention span can be very short indeed. Geminis are past-masters at knowing a little about a lot of subjects, which helps them to spout away and sound knowledgeable about all sorts of weird and wonderful topics. (It makes them born wheeler dealers, and these are the people who could sell ice to Eskimos or kangaroos to the Australians! Talk about the gift of the gab – they invented it!) As a result, they can flit from subject to subject or person to person in their constant quest for variety. Their boredom threshold is very low indeed, and the worst thing a Twin can say about someone is that they're a yawn a minute.

When it comes to work, a nine-to-five job where they know what's going to happen next is complete anathema to this lively lot. Being able to set their Timex by the time the tea trolley trundles round will give them the heebiejeebies faster than you can say 'Got any biscuits?'. Instead, they should opt for any occupation that doesn't keep them chained to a desk, especially if it concerns communication. Anything from journalism to selling encyclopaedias will be a winner for them, as they're definitely the kings and queens of the media. (Put a book in their hands and they're happy, and as for the telephone, you can never prise them off it. Some Twins talk to the speaking clock if there's no one else around!)

One thing Geminis are never short of is admirers, and with their wonderful wit, sparkling sense of fun, pert and pretty looks and the ability to charm the birds out of the trees (not to mention talking their way out of tight spots in a way that leaves you speechless with admiration) they can break hearts in every direction. Even when they have a permanent partner they can still find it fun to flirt, and Mercurial men can be real lady-killers!

When it comes to the sentimental side of life, these Gemini guys and gals can feel very frightened of their emotions. That means that amours can accuse them of being cold-hearted and callous, but they aren't really like that at all. They just enjoy standing on the sidelines and being impartial observers, though that can lead to them analysing all their feelings and working out what they mean, rather than simply enjoying them for what they are. If you've fallen for one of these fascinating folk you'll have to learn to be patient and coax those sweet nothings out of them with your understanding ways.

Geminis may seem very cool and confident on the surface, whilst underneath they'll be shaking like jellies. In fact, their nerves can really get the better of them, and they should try to calm down and not do so many things at the same time. (These are the people who can watch the telly, read a book, do their knitting and carry on a conversation all at once.) Watch a Gemini relaxing and you'll notice that even then they're twiddling their feet or fiddling with their hands or hair – they just can't keep still. If they want to make the best of themselves, they've got to learn to unwind properly and not keep going at all hours of the day and night, otherwise they'll really wear themselves out.

CANCER – 22 JUNE–23 JULY

Home sweet home! That's the motto engraved on the heart of every Cancerian, for these folk aren't happy unless they're safe and secure in their own little nests. You only have to think about those crustaceous creatures, crabs, who symbolise this sign, to see how true it is. They're always scampering back to their boulders and getting out of harm's way.

In fact, if you want the key to the Cancerian character then just look at one of these briny-bound beasties. On the outside crabs appear frightening, furious and fearsome, as they scowl at you and wave their pincers about in a menacing and moody manner. But inside their crusty coating is something succulent, soft, delicious and delectable. Now, Cancerians are just like that, because they conceal their soft centres by being cantankerous and crotchety, and are always on the look-out for trouble. It's not that they want a fight with anyone, but they're so defensive that they like to anticipate any problems that could pop up. They're the sort of folk who'll rush up to you and slap you round the

17

face before you've said a word, just in case you were going to be nasty! Then, if you really are horrid, they'll be pleased that they struck the first blow. Cancerians can see slights, insults and rejections where none exist, and get all worked up about nothing at all. There's no doubt that these folk can be very touchy, tetchy and testy.

Mysterious magical Mistress Moon rules the sign of the Crab, and just as she waxes and wanes, so a Cancerian's moods and emotions will ebb and flow. What's more, Cancer's the first of the three Water signs, and when you add those two facts together you come up with a stunningly psychic soul. Crabs are intuitive and sensationally sensitive to their surroundings, both good and bad, and can absorb an atmosphere the way a sponge soaks up water. That can be wonderful when they're with positive people but they'll get very depressed and disillusioned when they've got negative or nasty folk for their companions.

You don't have to know a Moony man or maid for long to realise that emotions cascade from them in a never ending fountain of feelings. Because they belong to the Water element, it's hardly surprising that tears can spring to their eyes over things other folk would laugh at. Sentimental old weepy films get even male Crabs reaching for their hankies and having a satisfying sob session.

Crabs love cameras, because they record all those magic moments for posterity (a favourite Cancerian word!). Most Cancerians will have myriads of photos of their loved ones around them. Because they're so full of warm emotions, once you've been given a place in the heart of your favourite Cancerian you could be there for life. Even so, unless you're one of the family (and blood is thicker than water for these chaps and chapesses), it may take you quite a while to prove your worth. Cancerians have magnificent memories, but as well as remembering the good times, Crabs can also store away all sorts of snubs, sarcasms, hurts and hassles. Scorpios remember things because they want to wreak their revenge, but Cancerians do it for protection, because they don't want to suffer in the same way ever again.

Love is one of the most important words in any self-respecting Crab's vocabulary, because these folk adore amour and are full of fervent feelings. Their stupendously strong need for security makes them fantastically faithful and, like Taureans, they could cling on to a relationship long after it's given up the ghost. They just can't bear to say goodbye, even if they know in their heart of hearts that it's for their own good. Instead, their innate tenacity will keep them clinging on to

18

partners who are far from perfect. Some Crabs can find it almost impossible to let go of anything, making them the biggest hoarders in the zodiac. You can open a Cancerian's cupboards and have your bonce bombarded by parcels of every bill they've ever received, and as for mementoes, keepsakes, treasures and childhood toys, they'll all be stashed away in a safe place. If they give anything away for jumble, they're almost bound to change their minds and buy it all back again!

It's vitally important for Cancerians to know they're truly cared for and loved, and if you're the passionate partner of a Moony amour, then you must remember to declare undying devotion at all hours of the day and night – and act as though you mean it! There's a magnificently maternal feeling to folk born under this sign, and even male Crabs will want to look after their loved ones and wrap them in a warm cocoon of cosseting care. It almost goes without saying that kids and Crabs are a captivating combination, and they make perfect parents. If they can't have any of their own, then they'll adopt them somehow or other and be a Mummy or Daddy that way. And talking of parents, they'll play a very important role in a Crab's life, whether they love or loathe 'em. If all's well in the family line-up, a Cancerian will try to live near the clan and see them as often as possible.

Having a happy home life is of paramount importance to all Crabs, because they need to know they can scamper back to their cosy nests. Their protective personalities make them excel at any occupation that involves caring for others, and because they're Cardinal, they can be very ambitious indeed. Anything domestic, from cooking and catering, to strengthening their links with the past by selling antiques, studying history or assembling their family tree will suit them down to the ground. Whenever anything upsets them it's their stomachs that affect them first, and they can be prone to anything from butterflies in their tums to ulcers and upsets. Still, they need only to call on their splendid sense of humour to get them through a bad patch and they'll be laughing!

LEO – 24 JULY–23 AUGUST

Lights, action, music! It's on with the lovely Leos, and what a stupendous show they make! They're the proud family of the zodiac, and they all feel regal and dignified to a delicious degree. After all, they're ruled by the super Sun, giver of all life, and they're symbolised by that beautiful beast the Lion, king of the jungle. No wonder this lot love being the centre of attention! What's more, Leos are imbued with an innately imperial influence, and they can be very aware of their own worth. They may even be too conscious of their calibre sometimes! It's no accident that Leo governs all things theatrical, as they adore being centre-stage, basking in the spotlight of everyone's attention. Of course, there's good and bad in every sign, and some Leos can monopolise every conversation (they do love the sound of their own voices!), whilst others are as quiet as mice on the surface. (Inside, of course, it could be quite another story!)

Sometimes, a Leo's sense of superiority can come to the fore, making them a little too big-headed, full of themselves and flamboyant for some people's tastes. The trouble is that they can't cope with faint-hearted folk, and long to chivvy them along. Most Leos want to be a leader who rules the roost – they know their place in the pecking order of life and it certainly isn't tagging along behind someone else! However, if they want to make the most of their powerful personalities, they've got to learn some give and take. Above all, they must avoid being pompous or patronising, as that will win them far more foes than friends.

There's a gorgeous generosity inside most Leos that's just waiting to jump out at the slightest opportunity. They adore handing out gifts and little surprises to their nearest and dearest, and they're always the very best that money can buy. A Leo's the sort of person who doesn't have a penny to their name but manages to borrow enough boodle to throw the party of a lifetime, where the champagne flows and there's more caviare than anyone can eat. If you ask them about it they'll tell you that they've got standards to keep up! The trouble is that all that generosity, magnanimity and benevolence can turn to swank and swagger, making it seem that the Leo's forking out left, right and centre just to show off and earn the respect of less well-off folk.

And whilst we're on the subject of negative Leo traits, some of the people belonging to this pride of Lions contain more hot air than a Montgolfier balloon. They'll convince you that nothing is too much trouble, they'll say that they'll get you tickets to see a show that's sold out for months ahead or you'll be promised the earth. Only when it's too late and nothing has materialised do you realise you've been had.

As you might have guessed by now, luxury, leisure and pleasure come high on a Leo's list of priorities. The tiniest peek inside a Lion's lair will confirm that only the best is good enough for these regal beings. If they can't afford to buy what they really want, they'd rather not have anything at all. (Remember, these are not folk who make do, or put up with second best!) Although they try to be moderate with their money, it doesn't take much for their extravagant exuberance to swing into action and send them straight round to the most expensive, ritzy and up-market shop they can find. Their sense of style means that they'd much rather buy all their bits and bobs from Harrods or somewhere similar, than the scruffy shop at the end of the street.

Whenever the holiday season comes around, these high-living Leos will hanker for the most prestigious place they can think of, where they can wallow in glorious grub and enjoy the stupendous scenery. What's more, these feline folk are so full of creative and artistic talents that they'll probably paint the breathtaking view from their hotel bedroom, do a dance to show how happy they are or ensure that the hills are alive with the sound of music. They're bursting with potential!

'Amour' is another Leonine word. The bit of the body ruled by this splendid sign is the heart, and some Leos have such titanic tickers it's terrific! Love is a many-splendoured thing for all these passionate pussycats, and when they fall for someone it's hook, line and sinker. There are no half measures for a Leo in Love. (Let's face it, there aren't usually any half measures for a Leo at all – they like having the works every time!) These loving lads and lasses won't leave their partner in any doubt about how they feel, and their Fiery natures and Sunny sensitivity help them to express their emotions in an eloquent and elegant, ardent and affectionate manner. A Leo in love is like a Lion with two tails, and the cat that got Cupid's cream!

Being one of the Fixed bunch in the heavens, Leos are lastingly loyal and trustworthy. But if they're feeling neglected or betrayed by their beloved, then they could look for comfort in someone else's arms. They hate to be rejected. In the astrological recipe, Lions were given a great big dollop of personal pride, which can be good or bad depending on how positive a pussycat they are. They're such a dignified bunch that sometimes they can miss out on an opportunity, or let go of a partner, because they won't allow themselves to be seen in an inferior, or poor, light. Even so, Leos who are without a darling of their very own should remember that there's more than one type of love, and friends and family can warm the cockles of their huge hearts just as much as an inamorata. Thanks to their Fiery element, their emotions are always waiting to flare up into a heartwarming blaze of amour! Just like real-life lions and lionesses, all these cuddly pussycats love toddlers, and will be puffed up with pride at the thought of having children of their very own.

It should come as no surprise by now to know that Leos excel at all things theatrical – as long as they play the lead, of course! But whatever trade they take up it must be one in which they can organise themselves, as they hate other people telling them what to do. As long as they can be their own bosses they'll be happy. What a smashing sight!

VIRGO – 24 AUGUST–23 SEPTEMBER

Perfection! That's the order of the day for these vestal Virgos, though there are a few of them who've fallen by the wayside and are too higgledy-piggledy for words. The majority, however, like to be perfect themselves first and then go on to everything (and everyone) around them. Sounds like a tall order, but these Mercurial marvels prove it can be done. These folk like to lead neat and tidy lives, and chaos and clutter can make them come over all unnecessary in ten seconds flat!

Because they're ruled by Mercury, that mental magician of the skies, Virgos are analytical, intelligent and cool, calm and collected. They love swotting up on their facts and knowledge. Unlike jumping-jack Geminis, who are also ruled by this mini marvel as well as sharing their Mutable quality (making them very versatile and adaptable), Virgos belong to the Earth element, so they keep their feet on the ground and are much more practical and pragmatic. The trouble is that sometimes they can be a bit too discriminating and detached for comfort, with the result that others find them offputting and offhand. That's when the negative side of the Virgoan nature comes to the fore, and they become too critical and carping for comfort.

The perfectionist Virgoan nature is great when it comes to work but not so hot in one-to-one affairs, as these Mercurial maids and men analyse everyone's behaviour and hand out black marks all round. Sometimes they act like Sherlock Holmes on overtime. 'What did that mean?' they'll wonder, as they put every action under their mental microscopes. When they start on themselves they can become too introverted for their own good, and then they'll be incredibly insular and inhibited. (Usually, the person they find the most fault with is themselves, when they can be very harsh critics indeed.) That's when they start up a vicious circle inside themselves, which could lead to all sorts of nervous ailments.

You can always tell a Virgoan's abode, 'cos it's so spick and span, with the cushions permanently plumped up, no bits of fluff on the floor or hankies behind the bed (but how do you know that?) and woodwork so shiny you can see your face in it. Even so, some Virgos inhabit homesteads that are so untidy it's like tackling an assault course every time you try to cross a room! Some signs postpone getting down to the housework for as long as possible, or pay someone else to do it (a Virgo, if they're clever!), but this lot positively revel in beating as they sweep as they clean. You see, the thought that a speck of dust or dirt is lurking in a corner fills them with horror and makes them break out in a cold sweat. They've got to get it before it gets them! Even when they go visiting they'll be like Yo-Yos as they leap up to straighten a picture on the wall (although only they can see that it's crooked), empty ashtrays or get on with the washing up at every opportunity. They don't think they're being rude, though, as neatness comes naturally to them, and it upsets their equilibrium to see anything untidy, dirty or grubby. In fact, even the Virgos who are messy wish they could whisk around with a dustpan and brush.

As far as these folk are concerned, health is wealth (ideally they'd like both, in equal measures!), and they can swallow so many pills, potions and powders for even the most minor ache or pain that they rattle when they walk. Browsing through a medical encyclopaedia can be disastrous, 'cos they'll soon convince themselves that they've got everything from alopecia to zinc deficiency. As for their first-aid kits, they're bound to be big, stuffed with every medicament known to man just in case they're afflicted by something strange. According to astrology, it's the intestines that are a Virgo's weak spot, and they often play up when these folk are feeling nervy or on edge. At the first hint of trouble from their tummies these pristine people make straight for the prunes or a bucket of bran to get the germs out of their systems as soon as possible.

The Earthy side of a Virgo's neat nature makes them most matter-of-fact, but one area they can find very off-putting is their emotions. Sometimes, they're really remote, distant and distracted. When love strikes, Mercury makes them wonder what it's all about, and they can be scared silly of committing themselves to someone. They may even censor what they say, because sweet nothings will sound soppy to their exacting ears. If you're their amour, the best thing to do is to woo them with some wine, but woe betide you if it brings on one of their heads! Pass the paracetamol!

Workwise, these vibrant Virgos are a wow! One thing they're not frightened of is hard slog, especially if they're wearing themselves out to help someone else. (Service is their middle name.) They'll dispense favours at every (good) turn and will gladly go miles out of their way to give someone a lift home. And their hankering for healthy living makes them marvels in all matters medical.

Anyone looking for a person who's diligent, dependable and dutiful should look no further than the nearest Mercurial boy or girl. They have a terrific talent for organisation, which means they make perfect PAs, or the sort of secretary who's utterly indispensable. Anything to do with figures fills them with fulfilment, because their minds operate in such a logical way that all things arithmetical are a positive pleasure to them, and one area in which they excel is accountancy. And because they're terrifically tidy, with an exacting eye for the tiniest detail and scrupulously shipshape in everything they do, fiddly work like designing or printing is right up their street.

As you'll have gathered, this Mercurial and Mutable mob don't suffer fools gladly, and although they'll always have their eyes peeled for a pretty face or a handsome hunk (they're not stupid!), they won't want to get to know anyone who's an idiot. So if you want to pal up with one of this likeable lot, you'd better swot up lots of knowledge and fascinating facts first!

LIBRA – 24 SEPTEMBER–23 OCTOBER

Whenever you can smell fragrant flowers, stunning scent or aromatic aftershave, you can bet that a Libran's not far behind. Wondering why? Well, this luscious lot are numero uno in the nasal ratings. They love to be surrounded by sweet smells (yes, that does include the blissful bouquet of success, but more about that later), and will spray on all sorts of perfumes to their heart's content. They always want to present the best side of themselves to the world, and some Librans are very vain Venusians on the quiet, and will spend hours practising their preening when no one is around to catch them. One of their favourite pastimes is sinking up to their shell-likes (which will be squeaky clean, of course) in a brimming bubble bath, with a long cool drink in one hand and their own true love in the other. (They'll be one and the same thing if one of these darlings is a dipsomaniac!)

Librans really do love all things bright and beautiful, which isn't surprising in the slightest when you realise that their ruling planet is Venus. She endows these fabulous folk with a love of harmony and a need for balance in every aspect of their existences. What's more, they belong to the sign of the Balance, and if they're to feel truly happy and perfectly in tune, their very own set of scales must be swinging in total symmetry. The trouble is that they're extremely sensitive souls, so it doesn't take much to set 'em bobbing about in different directions, and that can cause havoc and bring on one of the Libran's not so magnificent moods. They'll take everyone by surprise when that lollipop face, which is usually wreathed in sunny smiles, becomes furrowed by frowns, and a large Libran thundercloud hovers over their heads, threatening to burst at any minute. Luckily for the rest of us, those moods usually end as suddenly as they start (though some Venusians do stage the sulks in an Oscar-winning way), and the sun will come out again as they once more dispense their own balanced brand of bonhomie and beauty.

Peace at any price is the Libran motto, as the merest hint of a discord or disagreement gets them all of a doodah. As the second member of the trio of Air signs, Librans are intellectual and intelligent, but their ravishing ruler Venus makes them much more openly affectionate than their fellow signs of Gemini and Aquarius. They can both be rather detached, but Librans are more able to show their feelings, even though they don't necessarily wear their hearts on their sleeves. (Emotions may be seething away inside them, but on the surface they'll seem perfectly unruffled and unconcerned.)

Something else that sets Librans apart from the other Air signs is that they're always on the hunt for the perfect partner. Geminis seem to flit from one friend to another as the fancy takes them (if it's Wednesday it must be Wendy), and Aquarians often prefer to be alone (they've got no time for trivial types) but Librans are definitely happiest when in the company of convivial companions. Even when they're one half of a happy couple, they can't help wondering if they've yet to meet their real soulmate in life. (Poor you if you're the partner of one of these romantic roamers!) You see, they have very high expectations indeed when it comes to *affaire de coeur*, and it takes a supremely special someone to live up to them! Just to make matters worse, they can't bear being alone for long, and often fall into a relationship because it seemed to be the best option at the time, and now they can't face the thought of all the upsets and upheavals they'll cause if they call the whole thing off.

Falling in love with love is as easy as pie for this sentimental sign. They absolutely adore anything to do with romance, and their partners and paramours can look forward to being wined and dined, deluged with poems, presents and all the paraphernalia of love that Librans adore. However, all that devotion can mean that these Venusian love birds miss out when all their friends feel fed-up because they never see them any more – they want to spend all their spare time with their one true love. Librans can be very selfless sweethearts, always putting their partners first and forgetting about their own needs and desires, and that can mean that some unscrupulous or faithless folk can take terrible advantage of them.

Coming to a decision is the hardest thing in the world for Librans, as they can always see both sides of an argument. Even wondering whether to have tea or coffee can get them scratching their heads, so when it comes to weighing up the pros and cons of an important issue they don't stand an earthly! Making up their minds may take weeks (by which time everyone else will have long since lost patience with them), but once they've done it, usually there's no turning back.

Being Cardinal creatures, Librans are very good indeed at going after whatever it is they want from life, and normally get it by hook or by crook. Watch a Libran in action and you'll wonder if they can be that nice all the time. Want to know a secret? Well, Libra is the sign of the iron hand in the velvet glove, and sometimes these easy-going and pleasant people get their own way by being as sweet as pie on the surface and doggedly determined underneath!

The Libran need for partnership spills over into every area of their lives, and especially work. They do best when they're part of a team, whether that consists of two or twenty people. And their captivating charm and uncanny knack of coming out with the right word at the right time means that they're born diplomats. Jobs connected with the beauty business also appeal to their sense of style and love of glamour. What's more, because artistic ability is second nature to them, they need an occupation that makes the most of their creative skills and flair for design. The trouble is that they often run out of steam halfway through whatever it is they're doing, especially if they encounter snags, set-backs or hiccups galore. Even so, once they put their minds to it they can go very far indeed!

SCORPIO – 24 OCTOBER–22 NOVEMBER

What a misunderstood, misrepresented and misconstrued sign Scorpio is! Some folk think they're sex machines on legs (could that be wishful thinking, I wonder?), others that they're going to be stabbed in the back by the Scorpio's stiletto (and I don't mean their high heels!) and a few believe that they're spies who came in from the cold ready to sneak up on them when they least expect it.

26

So what's the real truth behind the Scorpio legend? Well, there's no doubt that they're very intense and complicated creatures, full of hidden depths and seething with strange psychological secrets. Folk can never get to the bottom of a Plutonian's personality: an enigma is the only way to describe them! There's much more to these people than meets the eye – just think of an iceberg bobbing along in a freezing sea; there's a little lump that can be seen on the surface, but most is hidden from view, only to be glimpsed now and then. Well, Scorpios are just the same, and equally inscrutable.

Two of the biggest and most powerful planets in the celestial scenario rule this sign – macho Mars and profound, pulverising Pluto. No wonder Scorpios have such a rocky reputation! This cosmic cocktail makes them full of atomic energy, single-minded determination, a will that's made of iron and magnetic personalities. Very often it's the eyes that are a Scorpio's strongest and most fascinating feature, and they can speak volumes. You'll know when these folk are feeling furtive because they'll peer their way through the biggest and blackest pair of sunglasses you've ever seen!

There are three sorts of Scorpios, ranging from the lowest of the low to the highest of the high. At the bottom is the Snake, who slithers about in the undergrowth of life and latches on to likely-looking victims like a poisonous parasite. Next in the line-up is the enterprising Eagle, who's always on the hunt for some adventure (remember James Bond?) and finally at the pinnacle of the Plutonian pecking order comes the Dove, who's searching for spiritual fulfilment. All the same, Scorpios are far more likely to be a blend of all three types rather than definitely a saint or decidedly a sinner. Don't forget that it's very difficult indeed to pin these people down!

Cancer, Scorpio and Pisces make up the three Water signs, all of whom are renowned for their emotional natures. Scorpios never forget, just like their cousins the Crabs, though it's for rather a different reason. You see, Scorpios will plot and plan their revenge for years on end if they've suffered a slight, and will wait until the time is right before moving in for the kill. To give even more force to their retentive memories, they're part of the Fixed celestial section, endowing them with intensity, immutability and intransigence. Once a Scorpio's taken offence, there'll be no going back or changing their minds! However, what they may not realise until it's too late is that their policy of getting even at all costs can be very destructive indeed – and self-destruction is the big bugbear of these powerful people. Let's face it, they can reach the heights but they can also plumb the depths, with only themselves to blame when they come to grief.

Pluto exerts phenomenal power over its Scorpionic subjects, giving them an atomic intensity, and Mars can fill them with some very physical feelings. Add the two together and there's the celebrated Scorpio sex drive! All the same, this is the sign of extremes, compulsions and obsessions, so whilst some of these folk are always up to sexy fun and games, there are others born under this sign who are fundamentally frightened of the very thought of anything spicy, saucy and salacious. Odd, isn't it?

Just like the snake shedding its skin, or the phoenix rising from its ashes, Scorpios excel at casting off their previous existences and starting all over again on a more vibrant and vital path. That's because this is the sign of life and death, and whatever happens, the Scorpio's tremendous willpower, resolution and unbending backbone will see them through. Their stunning sense of discipline will help them clamber up the ladder of success, learning important lessons along the way. Amongst the perfect Plutonian professions are detective work or even being a spy. There's nothing this lot like better than keeping a few secrets, dabbling in espionage or even some undercover work (back to bed?). Psychiatry may also appeal to some Scorpios, as their X-ray vision and intuitions can help them penetrate straight to the heart of a problem.

If there's one thing that Scorpios strive for it's control, whether they've got the whip hand over themselves or other people. They don't want to wield their power in full view of everyone, but prefer to manipulate it behind the scenes, using it in a tactical way. And it won't just be at work – these are the folk who can wage psychological warfare with loved ones till the cows come home. They need to know that they're the boss, but they should be on their guard that their lust for complete control doesn't get the better of them, or sting them like a scorpion.

A strong sense of loyalty is one of the most endearing Scorpio traits. Something they have to watch like a hawk is the green-eyed monster, as these passionate Plutonians can be overwhelmed by black bouts of jealousy, suspicion or possessiveness that can wreak havoc in all directions. Once they've got a whiff of their partner being up to no good they'll leave no stone unturned till they've been proved right or wrong. To make matters worse for their unsuspecting sweethearts, they've got a line of questioning that makes the Spanish Inquisition look like a tea party. What complex, compulsive but fascinating folk these Scorpios are!

SAGITTARIUS – 23 NOVEMBER–21 DECEMBER

They say that it's better to travel hopefully than to arrive, but Sagittarians love doing both. These are the roamers and wanderers of the zodiac, and lots of them are never happier than when travelling to pastures new.

These rovers are ruled by that jolly giant Jupiter, who injects them with a very restless streak indeed. They love being on the move, even if it's just mentally when they put those brilliant brains through their paces with an improving book. Another proverb is that knowledge is power, and all these Archers would agree with that one hundred per cent. They have a thirst for learning that can never be quenched because they're well aware of all the subjects, topics and facts they haven't even begun to discover yet. It makes some of them feel very inferior or frustrated.

Many of these cerebral Saggys aren't comfy or content unless they're surrounded by books, and they'll spend all their spare time reading everything they can lay their hands on, from thrillers to theology, mysteries to mystics, philosphies to foreign lingos. They love to know what makes the world go round, and reading about religions, creeds, codes and cultures opens their eyes to new schools of thought and gives them plenty to think about.

Being the third of the Fire signs, and Mutable to boot, means that Sagittarians are full of energy, and don't like things to stay stagnant for too long. And that includes themselves. The world (and in a few years it'll be the universe too!) is full of Archers with knapsacks on their backs trotting around trying to experience as many sights and sounds as possible before it's time to head for home. As a result, they've got to get the wanderlust out of their souls before they settle down to an ordered existence or become one half of a domestic duo, otherwise they'll find themselves in big trouble. You see, these Centaurs need to know that their lives are versatile and variable, and the sense of being tied down or trapped in one place is likely to make them break out in a cold sweat and try to escape from their prospective prison as soon as possible.

These are the folk who can vanish from your life for years on end, as they trek about the other side of the world amassing experiences the way other people collect stamps. Even the Sags who stay at home and just indulge in armchair travel could find that they know lots of people from different walks of life, or fall for a foreigner and eventually emigrate to a sunnier climate. Not surprisingly, when it comes to jobs anything connected with travel can be a winner for these footloose folk, and publishing can also see them go far.

Make no mistake, this is a very high-minded sign. Many Sagittarians can be very spiritual souls indeed, and may decide to combine their love of travel with their religious beliefs by becoming missionaries or evangelists. Even if they're perfectly happy living in Liverpool they'll still enjoy discussing the meaning of life with friends and philosophers.

It's just as well that enterprising, expansive and expensive Jupiter is the guiding light of all these Archers, because he's also the planet of luck, and some of these Sags seem to lead charmed lives. Let's face it, they need every ounce of good fortune they can find, as they're always knocking things over, tripping over their feet or falling flat on their faces! They're also very good at putting their feet in it at every opportunity, and they can be brilliant at dropping bricks, making *faux pas* or embarrassing everyone around them. Some Sags seem to get it wrong every time! Luckily, good-natured Jupiter also injects them with an overwhelmingly optimistic outlook in life, thereby helping them to surmount any obstacles placed in their paths and see something positive in even the worst calamities or crises. What's more, they're usually right! Not for nothing are they the sign of the Archer. It shows that they're always aiming straight for the stars, and although they often miss their target by miles, whenever they get a bull's-eye they'll be crowned with glory.

Perhaps it's their experiences of making mistakes that does it, but whatever the reason, Centaurs are marvellous at listening to other people's problems and getting them back on the right road. They're full of words of wisdom, for they are truly the philosophers of the astrological dozen. However, be warned, for they can be breathtakingly blunt at times, and can always be relied on to say exactly what they think. If there's one thing they hate it's hypocrisy, and they loathe the thought of telling lies or fibs. So next time you ask a Sagittarian their opinion about your new frock or face lift, brace yourself for their utterly honest reply!

Thanks to their Fiery temperaments, Archers vibrate with verve and vigour, love having a good laugh and can be angry one minute and back to normal the next. Their happy-go-lucky approach to life spills over into matters of the heart, making them bright and breezy amours, but they can show their very independent natures even when they've met their one true love. Some of them will be fantastically faithful, but there are a few who'll still have lots of emotional escapades even when they've plighted their troth.

Not being able to sit still for more than a few minutes at a time, sporty and athletic activities are right up a Centaur's street. Lots of them have lovely long legs or strong thighs, and will walk up hill and down dale at a spanking pace. Horses have a special appeal to many Archers (so does gambling on them down at the bookie's or at the race track!), though they love all their furry and four-legged friends, and the feeling's probably entirely mutual, for who can resist a sunny Saggy?

CAPRICORN – 22 DECEMBER–20 JANUARY

Gregarious, gorgeous and genial or grouchy, grumpy and gross? Ask folk what they think of Capricorns and they'll come up with all sorts of answers. You see, like Scorpios, the poor old Goats get a very raw deal in the astrological stakes, with many people completely misunderstanding them or giving them a wide berth. They obviously don't know what they're missing.

It can be a laugh a minute with this lovable lot. Their sardonic humour and that wonderful wit that's as dry as a bone will get all their family and friends splitting their sides with laughter. That's one side of the Capricorn coin, and very shiny it is too. However, the next day that Goat will be as gloomy and glum as a wet weekend, showing the other facet of the Capricornian character. It's all because they're ruled by stern Saturn, the old age pensioner of the planets, and he exerts a very intense influence over his subjects indeed. Remember that Saturn is surrounded by rings? Well, in astrology those rings restrict Capricorns in all sorts of ways, holding them back, tying them down and even making them feel inferior. One thing's for sure – they're not rings of confidence! Goats are such shy, self-effacing souls that they're usually backwards in coming forwards and some of them have inferiority complexes so large that they never dare ask for anything in case they're refused or rejected. (A very fundamental fear for all Goats.)

Because they're the last of the three Earth signs, Capricorns have always got their tootsies on terra firma, and they view the world through very realistic eyes (no rose-coloured glasses for this lot!). The symbol of this sign may be the Goat, but that's only half the story. You see, some of them are perfectly happy to prance about in the pasture, leading a peaceful life, making ends meet and staying out of trouble. But some of them are very resourceful ruminants indeed, who scamper straight up the sides of the mountain and don't stop till they've reached the top (these are the giddy Goats!). It may take some time (success usually comes late in life for cautious Capricorns), but they'll get there in the end. What ambitious wee beasties they are, but what else could they be since they're Cardinal creatures? That means that when they're playing in life's lottery they go for the star prize every time.

Everyone has emotions, but often a Capricorn's sensitivities are buried deep beneath a staid and serious surface, 'cos they're too frightened to let them out. (There's always the danger of them being horrendously hurt, or even laughed at, and a Goat will go to any lengths to avoid anything as unpleasant as that.) It could be a different matter altogether when it comes to sex as it'll be no holds barred (literally!), thanks to their Earthy and erotic natures. You know what they say about old Goats! Any inamoratas who are waiting to be deluged with warm words of love, surrounded by hearts and flowers or swept off their feet in a ravishing rush of romance will be deeply disappointed by their Capricorn Cupid. If their amour asks them if they love 'em, this Saturnine sweetheart will reply, 'Well, I live with you, don't I?', and that'll be as far as they're prepared to go in the sentimental stakes. Let's face it, these gorgeous Goats will never set the world on fire with their passionate protestations!

What they can offer, though, is long-lasting love, loyalty and a lifetime of being looked after. Capricorn men take being the bread-winner very seriously indeed, and they'll be diligent and dutiful in bringing home the bacon and ensuring that their families have everything they need.

Prestige, honour and acclaim are all in the top ten of a Capricorn's ambitions, but they need their achievements to be seen, and they have to be convinced that their peers, superiors and subordinates really respect and revere them. You'll find gaggles of Goats running local councils, being big bosses or senior civil servants, because they love responsibility. In fact, they lap it up, and one of their biggest hates is delegating to others. They'd much rather do every job themselves, because even if it takes all night they'll know they've done it properly. (Capricorns are often a weeny bit wary of trusting people, in case they're let down.)

Becoming a workaholic is a trap many Goats fall into, and if they're not careful they can ruin the relationship with their other half because they're never around! Instead, they'll be burning the candle at both ends or bringing their work home with them until it drives their darling round the bend – or into the arms of someone else. Even so, Goats are wonders at work, and they're so punctual (they hate wasting anything, but especially time) that people could set their watches by their comings and goings.

Don't think it's all plain sailing for these go-getting Goats, because it isn't. Instead, their rigorous ruler Saturn makes sure that he places lots of pitfalls and problems in their paths, so that they can learn from their mistakes. They'll have a struggle at first, but it'll turn them into wonderfully wise folk. And anyway, from their forties onwards, those Capricorn fortunes can take a sudden change for the better and from then on they start making up for lost time. What's more, the older a Goat gets, the better their life will become. Other folk age as the years roll on, but the extraordinary thing about Capricorns is that they start off old and get younger and younger, till they're skipping about like spring lambs at a time when their contemporaries are collapsing into wheelchairs!

Keeping up appearances is what it's all about for careful and conservative Capricorns, as they like to be seen at their best at all times. They're often racked by worries about what the neighbours think, and their lack of self-confidence means that they're always trying to show the most favourable or impressive side of themselves. These modest mortals can find it almost impossible to believe that folk like them for what they are, with or without all the trappings of success, but you don't have to know a Capricorn for long before you fall under their smashing spell. They're so wise, witty and wry!

AQUARIUS – 21 JANUARY–19 FEBRUARY

Whether they're ruled by unusual and unconventional Uranus or steadied by sane and secure Saturn, one thing's for certain –Aquarians are a law unto themselves! This is the most weird and wonderful of the twelve signs, and all Aquarians have one thing in common – they're not like anyone else in the zodiac!

Once you meet one of these fascinating folk, the first thing to decide is which of their two planets has the upper hand. If they seem rather cautious and careful, then turn to the Capricorn section and read all about those Saturnine souls. On the other hand, if they're wacky, way-out and wild, then settle down for some illuminating information about these Uranian marvels. Even so, all Aquarians will take you by surprise sometimes, so don't imagine that a Saturn-styled Water Carrier will always act like a Capricorn, 'cos every now and then they'll do something that will completely take you by surprise. As for the lot ruled by Uranus, you'd better always expect the unexpected and then you'll be prepared for almost every eventuality! Don't ever forget that Aquarians are way ahead of their time.

This is definitely the sign of the innovator, and you only need know that such cleverclogs as Galileo were born under astounding Aquarius to realise what brilliant brainboxes, incredible inventors and galvanising geniuses these people can be. Because they're the third and last of the Air signs, they're very intellectual, intelligent and innovative. Silly or superficial folk leave them cold, as they've got no time for them at all. Some of these Airy individuals can be as cool as a summer breeze, detached and disinterested from the world around them and apparently more concerned with the workings of their minds than matters of the heart. Water Carriers may be celibate and solo for years on end and not give it a thought, and then suddenly they'll go on a randy rampage that'll really set the tongues a-wagging and the curtains a-twitching. The trouble is that love leaves lots of these clever creatures speechless – through perplexity, not pleasure! They're not sure what it's all about, and the thought of being swept off their feet by unbridled lust makes them want to run in the opposite direction as fast as their legs will carry them.

Whenever an Aquarian does think about pairing up, they've got to make quite sure that their beloved is a pal first and foremost. You see, friendships count for a great deal where a Water Carrier's concerned, and they need to know that their other half is also their best buddy. What's more, sex and Aquarians doesn't always go together, and if the passion peters out, there's got to be something deeper and longer-lasting to hold this twosome together. Aquarians find brains much more bewitching than bodies, so as long as there's still some mental magic everything should be fine.

Something every potential paramour of an Aquarian should know is that if there's one thing they hate it's being tied down. It's not that they're going to run off with someone else, but any hint of a romantic restriction, demand to know where they've been or attempt to clip their wings will result in a very sticky situation indeed. For a start, once they've paired up for life, a Water Carrier will still want to carry on seeing all their friends, and their other half may not take kindly to that idea at first. However, as far as an Aquarian's concerned, their companion's got to like it or lump it, because their pals play a very important role in their world.

If you're having problems coming to terms with your Uranian's host of chums, then here's something to cheer you up. Loyalty is high on an Aquarian's list of priorities, and that's not surprising when you realise that they belong to those Fixed and faithful folk. They aren't likely to run off with anyone else because that would break their code of honesty, truth and straightforwardness.

The trouble is that this steadfast side of their natures can clash loudly with their need for constant change. So whilst the Fixed side of an Aquarian is looking for a solid set-up, their Aquarian and Uranian side is being provocative and rocking the boat. You must remember that Aquarians are past masters at being shocking, controversial and avant-garde, but often they only do it to provoke a reaction. They love to astound everyone and then see what will happen next. A less outré and outrageous aspect of their fixity can lead to some very stubborn viewpoints, with the Aquarian digging in their heels over a question or sticking like glue to what they believe in.

If there's one thing guaranteed to get an Aquarian tearing their hair out with frustration and fury it's the merest hint of some red tape. Bigwigs, people in power and officious officials can all make a Water Carrier's blood pressure shoot up in two seconds flat, and only increase their determination to get the better of their bureaucratic bugbear – and they will, sooner or later! If they want to feel fulfilled at work they must choose a career in which they're not restricted in any way. Being self-employed or running their own business is perfect for them, as another thing they can't abide is being told what to do. They're far too independent, visionary and unique for that. All hell will be let loose if they have a job that involves filling in forms or signing things in triplicate ('Why?', the Water Carrier will want to know, before tearing everything in two).

Like-minded folk love the zany Aquarian sense of humour and will enjoy chumming up with one of these puzzling people just to see what they'll say or do next. With their forward-thinking minds and talents for looking into the future, Aquarians make tremendous trend-setters and can set off fashions without even knowing it. Some of them, though, are so quirky and cranky that they'll adopt an attitude or wear a wardrobe that went out with the ark. But whether your Aquarian is trendy or trapped in a time warp, you'll find them inspiring and intriguing for ever more. Smashing!

PISCES – 20 FEBRUARY–20 MARCH

What puzzles these Piscean people are! Think of the amazing assortment of fish swimming about in the seven seas and you'll have a good idea of how many different Fishy folk there are. That's because Pisces is one of the most complicated and contrary signs in the celestial set-up, full of mysterious motivations, fervent feelings and strange sentiments. What's more, this is the last of the twelve Sun signs, and also the last of the three Water signs, so all these Fishes have been given an extra helping of spiritual sensibilities, strong sympathies and strange insights.

All the Water signs are endowed with everlasting emotion, but these Fishy folk have a double dose. They're also supremely psychic, intensely intuitive and receptive to all sorts of atmospheres, influences and images that pass other, less aware, people by. Netfuls of these perceptive Pisceans make marvellous mediums, because they can easily tune in to the higher vibes. Even if they only get them once in a blue moon, all Fishes should act on their hunches or flashes of inspiration – they could be surprised at how well they pay off! Like their Cancerian counterparts, Pisceans can tune in to the atmosphere around them in the same way as a radio and that's lovely when they're with high-minded folk, but they should be especially careful when they meet sinister, weird or even evil people, or they'll be drained, depressed, debilitated or deceived. Because they're Mutable mortals, Pisceans are like chameleons, altering their attitudes or switching their speech according to their surroundings and what they think is expected of them.

Being Mutable makes them dual creatures and gives them two halves to their natures – hence the symbol of this sign, which is a pair of fish swimming in opposite directions. Sometimes these two sides can clash and create inner conflict, or they can mean that the Fish says (and means) something one minute, only to completely change their minds and morals half an hour later. As a result, they can get the reputation for being unreliable, untrustworthy or even out-and-out liars, even though all three accusations may be unfair and untrue.

For a few, the line between fact and fiction can become blurred and blunted when they confuse what's really happening with a big dollop of

wishful thinking. Others of this sign are much more matter of fa[ ]
philosophical about life, making them like sage Sagittarians rather than
foggy Fishes. That's because this sign has two rulers – notoriously
nebulous Neptune and cut and dried Jupiter. If you want to know about
Pisceans who take life in their stride, then turn to the section on
Sagittarians, but if you know a Fish who's much more complex and
confusing than that, then they're ruled by Neptune, god of the sea.

One of the dangers lying in wait for these tantalising Fishes is
deception. They often don't have to worry about other people pulling
the wool over their eyes because they're so good at doing it themselves!
These folk can really fool themselves into thinking all sorts of weird and
wonderful things. Although positive Pisceans will indulge in delicious
daydreams whilst knowing that they're not real, some Fishes can spin
a web of wonderment around themselves until the fantasy factor takes
over completely and they're lost in a world of their own. They may even
help that self-deception along with drink or drugs, which will make
things even more woolly and unworldly. In fact, quite a few Fishes lead
a double existence, either in their imaginations or in real life, as they
indulge in all sorts of escapist fantasies and imaginings.

With such fertile imaginations, it's no wonder that Pisceans are
blessed with copious creative capabilities too. They're marvels in artistic
matters and even if they can't show off their own skills and talents
they'll certainly appreciate the attributes of others. They make divine
dancers, perfect poets, breathtaking beauticians and accomplished
actors, as well as being adept at anything associated with oil, refinement
and glamour.

What's more, they're so sensitive and philanthropic that these Fishes
have a captivating capacity for caring for others. You can find shoals of
patient Pisceans working for charities, in voluntary services and giving
their all in hospitals, prisons and other institutions. They'll happily do
good works without wanting any reward, though they have to protect
themselves from getting too wrapped up in other people's problems. It's
only too easy for them to get bogged down by the cares and woes of
others, and another possible pitfall is when unscrupulous folk take
advantage of them. These sympathetic Pisceans can fall for a sob story
at the drop of a hankie, and they may find themselves giving away time,
sentiments or money to someone who isn't really a deserving case at all.

As a Water sign, a Piscean's emotions know no bounds, and they
overflow with love for friends and family, amours and amigos.
However, they can be their own worst enemies when it comes to matters

of the heart, telling themselves that their other half truly loves them when really they know they're being unfaithful with everyone in the street, or even conducting an imaginary relationship with someone who barely knows that they exist! Other Fishes can get in a fluster and give into fears, phobias and psychosomatic illnesses all because their beloved's been too busy to be with them lately, or even 'cos they enjoy acting the martyr and putting on a self-sacrificing or selfless show. Some of these Fishes can be very neurotic indeed.

Pisceans need to be in places that are calm and serene, otherwise their finely tuned nervous system is jarred. It can make them feel quite ill to be around folk who are aggressive, oppressive or suggestive, and the more beautiful and benign their surroundings, the happier and more content these complicated but compelling Pisceans will be. Anything elegant, enchanting or entrancing should be just what the doctor ordered!

RUSSELL'S RELATIONSHIP GUIDE

AQUARIUS MAN AND ARIES WOMAN

It's terrific! You two really know how to keep each other guessing, and love the unpredictable and unconventional atmosphere when you're together. Because your Arian amourette doesn't like it when things are too easy for her (that would be boring!), she adores being with you, because who knows what you'll do next? You may take a sudden vow of celibacy or decide to take a crash course in how to be a Casanova, but whatever you do, it won't be predictable. Honesty is a quality that will play an important role in your relationship, as neither of you can bear lying, deceit or duplicity. In fact, you can both be a bit blunt and brusque in your strivings to be honest, but you certainly won't keep any secrets from each other, and because jealousy isn't a problem between you, you can both go off and do your own things whenever you want. Perfect!

AQUARIUS MAN AND TAURUS WOMAN

What a dogmatic duo you are! You're both as stubborn as mules and immovable as mountains, which can spell disaster when the two of you get together. It's very difficult indeed for you to sort out any disagreements or dilemmas because neither of you can appreciate any viewpoint but your own! One area where you can really clash and come to grief is in amour, 'cos you've got very different expectations indeed. As an emotional Bullette, your amour needs lots of love and affection

39

from her other half, plus a sensuous and sultry sex life, but that could be the last thing you've got in mind. For a start, you'll find her possessive and jealous ways very hard to handle, and whenever you want to go off by yourself for a few hours she won't like it one bit! You may also find it difficult to show your fond feelings, and you could both discover that this is a partnership that's full of problems.

AQUARIUS MAN AND GEMINI WOMAN

Splendiferous! It's a smashing set-up when you fall for a Gemini girl because you've got so much in common it's incredible. Some folk may find you too much to cope with, but your Mercurial maiden will welcome all your unconventional ideas, avant-garde attitudes and dazzling doings with open arms. At last she's found someone who couldn't be dull if they tried, and you'll think the same about her. You're evenly matched emotionally too, because you both belong to the Air element, which means you like to keep things light-hearted and lively – no steamy scenes for you Airy amours! Even so, don't fall into the trap of being frightened to show your feelings for each other, or things could turn from captivating into clinical. The more deep discussions and spirited set-tos you have about every subject under the sun, the happier you'll be, so chat away!

AQUARIUS MAN AND CANCER WOMAN

As chums you're a charming couple, but it can be quite another story if it's love that's brought you together, because you couldn't be more different emotionally if you tried. There's nowt your Crabette likes better than cuddling up close to the one she loves (that's you!), enfolding you in the warm cocoon of her love and spending the rest of your days tucked up together in your wee nest. The trouble is that the very idea of all that could send you scampering off in the opposite direction as fast as your legs can carry you. What's more, your views on sex may leave her open-mouthed in amazement or dumbfounded with disgust, just before the tears start trickling down her cheeks. You've both got to put your feelings into words, though you may still find it very hard to understand each other.

AQUARIUS MAN AND LEO WOMAN

Ten out of ten! That's how you rate on the compatibility scale, which is hardly surprising 'cos you're astrological opposites, and you know how opposites attract! Once you switch from friends to lovers, though, your

Leo lady might have to change her mind about you when she discovers that you're not as openly affectionate, ardent and amorous as she'd like. She adores being bowled over by demonstrations of passion and undying love, but she could wait a very long time before you behave like a latter-day Rudolph Valentino. Instead, your extremely erratic emotions are likely to be lecherous one moment and laidback the next. If you want your partnership to last, you'll have to show your lust and love more openly, and your Leo lass must learn to live with your brand of Aquarian amour. Persevere with this pairing and you'll be delighted with the ravishing results!

AQUARIUS MAN AND VIRGO WOMAN
What a difficult duo! Unless you're strongly Saturnalian, making you act like a Capricorn chap, this pairing could be a one-minute wonder, as you've got almost nowt in common. Your Virgoette's houseproud habits and desire for detail could soon drive you into a frenzy of frustration, and your unconventional and outré actions will have the same effect on her! Even sexually, you're poles apart, and the way you can change from chasing her to being chaste yourself can make the neat little head of your Virgoan valentine spin like a top. She needs to know where she stands in the romantic stakes, but she might be forever ignorant with you, thanks to your bedazzling behaviour. Keeping your partnership on a platonic plane could be your best bet if you want to stay in touch with this Mercurial maid, unless you're both prepared to work very hard indeed.

AQUARIUS MAN AND LIBRA WOMAN
Fine as friends but problematic as partners, that's the prognosis for this pairing. You both belong to the Airy element of the zodiac, so you share the need for an amour who's more than just a pretty face, but that could be where the resemblance ends. Being ruled by voluptuous Venus, your Libran lass rates love as number one on her list of priorities, whereas you may have lots of other interests and involvements that you consider to be just as important. What's more, there's nothing she likes better than a cosy kiss and cuddle, especially when it's helped along by some soft lights and sweet music, but you may only give her a peck on the cheek before rushing off to meet some mates and save the world. It's not that you don't care – just that you've got a funny way of showing it! If you want this relationship to work then you'll both have to make a real effort to understand each other's dreams and desires.

AQUARIUS MAN AND SCORPIO WOMAN

Better wrap up warm if you want this relationship to last, otherwise the emotional freeze between you will chill you both to the bone. The trouble is that your sensuous Scorpionette is suffused with strong sentiments and intense intentions, but you can be so unresponsive, undemonstrative and unemotional that you'll bring out all the very coldest parts of her personality. If you get as far as the bedroom she could feel spurned and slighted (watch out!) if you aren't as seductive, sensational and sexually insatiable as she'd like, because you simply won't feed her need for lots of love and affection. In return, you may find her far too demanding, demonstrative and difficult to deal with, and her attempts to tie you down (literally, luv?) and keep track of your every movement will just make you feel suffocated, stifled and stagnant. It may be almost impossible to make this twosome work.

AQUARIUS MAN AND SAGITTARIUS WOMAN

The truth, the whole truth and nothing but the truth – that's the way you'll run your relationship with a Sagittarian dame. After all, if there's one thing neither of you can stand it's the slightest suspicion of lies, dishonesty, insincerity or hypocrisy, so there's no danger of the two of you mincing your words or playing your cards close to your chest. Instead, you're more likely to be brutally frank and say exactly what you think, with no thought for sparing each other's blushes! You're very forward thinking but you can be a bit stubborn sometimes. Even so, your Archerette is usually able to jolly you out of your obstinate moods and keep you guessing, thanks to her vivacious and vibrant ways. You'll always have plenty to talk about, and your light and airy appetite for amour will mean you're magnificently matched when it comes to your emotions. There's no doubt about it – you're soul mates!

AQUARIUS MAN AND CAPRICORN WOMAN

What a dynamic duo! As long as you don't get bogged down in tradition, ruts or routines, the two of you could have a grand time together. If you're strongly Saturnine then you'll find you've got stacks in common, but even if you're a Uranian *homme* it won't be the end of the world. Your girl Goat has got to take your controversial, contrary and cranky characteristics in her stride, and resist any temptation to turn into a clinging vine emotionally, in case she's left all alone. If you're ruled by sane Saturn, then you'll have lots of Capricorn traits, but even so you'll love a whiff of excitement, and if there's none to be found then you'll do something outrageous just to see what happens. Your Capricorn Cupid's eyebrows may shoot straight off her head at some of the antics you get up to, but one thing's for sure – you'll keep her laughing!

AQUARIUS MAN AND AQUARIUS WOMAN

Now, the first thing for you two to work out is whether you're ruled by ungovernable Uranus or toe-the-line Saturn. If one of you is especially Saturnine then you should read the previous pairing of Aquarius and Capricorn, but if you're both influenced by unusual Uranus then you'll either be inseparable or at such loggerheads that you'll avoid each other like the plague! The minute you meet you'll know whether you're going to get on or not, though if you do pair up permanently it could cause thrills and spills all round as your mutual mates may be convinced that really you can't stand the sight of each other. What they won't realise is that taking your relationship at face value may be a big mistake, and that just because your desires or demonstrations of devotion are different from theirs, doesn't mean that you aren't happy together. Never mind, 'cos you'll both adore creating ripples and rumours with your shock tactics!

AQUARIUS MAN AND PISCES WOMAN

If you're more Saturnine than Uranian, then this could be a splendid set-up, but if you're truly Aquarian there may be troubled times ahead when you pair up with a Piscean girl. The first thing for you to realise about this Fishy female is that she adores romance, lives for love and likes her life to be as rhapsodic, imaginative and enriching as possible, and that could be a tall order for as unconventional a chap as you. Even if you can cater to her emotional appetite, after a while you could find her slightly too salacious, saucy and sexy for your tastes, though you'll be intrigued at first. If you want this pairing to work, then you've got to cultivate a more tender, tactile and treasuring approach, whilst she's got to come down to earth a bit and stop expecting you to act like Prince Charming every hour of the day. Then, you could live happily ever after!

AQUARIUS WOMAN AND ARIES MAN

Fun all the say, that's what you can expect when you team up with a lively Arian chap. Your original ways will always keep him on his toes, and although that could get some folk tearing out their hair with

43

frustration, he'll love every madcap moment of it! One minute you'll be acting like a demure damsel and the next you'll be the sexiest, most seductive siren he's ever seen. Even if you decide to ring the changes by turning celibate for a wee while he'll still be captivated and intrigued by your astonishing actions. Something else that he'll like is the way you never ask him where he's been or what he's been doing, and you'll expect the same no-questions-asked attitude from him. Your friends may wonder how you stick together, but you'll know – you're completely captivated by each other!

AQUARIUS WOMAN AND TAURUS MAN

If you're the sort of Aquarian lass who stands her ground, then you've more than met your match when you team up with a boy Bull. You're both past masters at sticking to your guns and refusing to alter your opinions, but unless you can both learn to compromise you'll never get anywhere. Let's face it, you won't agree on anything, whether it's what time to have your tea or where to go for your holidays! This could be a very problematic pairing indeed, especially if you're both intransigent, intractable and downright bloody-minded! You may also think your Taurean chap is too bovine and boring for words, whilst he finds your outré and outrageous ways a wee bit frightening or intimidating. Make no mistake, this relationship will never be plain sailing, but you're both such strong characters that maybe that's the very thing that'll keep you together!

AQUARIUS WOMAN AND GEMINI MAN

Anything goes! There are no holds barred when you embark on a perfect pairing with a Gemini chap, and you'll find each other full of fun and fascination. The way you lead your lives could set tons of tongues wagging as you both like doing your own thing, and it may even be your Mercurial male who stays at home with the wee ones whilst you earn the daily bread. (That's right – it's mother's pride!) You've got lots in common but one thing you won't see eye to eye about is honesty. As a glib Gemini, your amour can chat his way out of almost any tight spot and dabble in double talk that leaves folk feeling confused and confounded, but that won't appeal to honest you one iota. You believe in sticking to the facts, and can be so blunt and brusque that you sound really rude! So your mendacious male shouldn't be surprised if you succeed where others have failed and squeeze the truth out of him!

AQUARIUS WOMAN AND CANCER MAN

The more you two can talk to each other, the better your relationship will be, for communication is the key to your success. You see, because you're poles apart in so many ways, you can completely misunderstand each other's motives and minds unless you're able to talk about what you both need and want from life and love. You make fantastic friends, and there's usually a belly laugh or two just around the corner because you both adore a good giggle, but unless you're careful the problems can start when love blossoms between you. You'll find your Cancerian chap's innate sentimentality and sensitivity fascinating at first, but you may decide that you can have too much of a good thing after a while. On the other hand, he could find that your wild and wacky ways are too independent and indomitable for his taste. Even so, once you're tucked up in bed, or wherever else your lust leads you, you'll soon forget your differences in the heat of the moment!

AQUARIUS WOMAN AND LEO MAN

Ain't life grand? That's what you'll be saying when you fall for a Leo lad, and who can blame you? There'll be a daringly dramatic and thoroughly theatrical feeling when you two get together, and you're so well-suited that you could have started off as childhood chums and discovered as adults that life wasn't worth living without each other. Your unpredictable, imaginative and original actions and anything-goes attitudes will always keep your Leo lover on his toes, and he'll gladly let you do your own thing – as long as he knows you'll always return to his warm and welcoming arms. (You must remember that he's a very faithful and fervent feline fella!) Even so, unless he can take it in his stride when you blow hot and cold in the boudoir, you could hit some snags and setbacks if you're not careful. If you say you're having a celibate week, there's no doubt that you mean it and your Leo Lothario will have to wait for the seven days to pass, in the hopes that next time you could be feeling very hot-blooded indeed!

AQUARIUS WOMAN AND VIRGO MAN

Sorry? Pardon? What? When you two get together for an amorous alliance your conversation will be crammed with questions like these, 'cos you may as well be speaking in a foreign language for all the understanding and unity you'll have. In fact, you'll do much better as platonic pals than passionate paramours, because then you can put the world to rights or discuss all sorts of subjects and topics with no trouble

45

at all. It's when your emotions pop up that you'll hit the hiccups. If you're ruled by splendid Saturn then you'll have much more in common, but if you're driven by unruly Uranus your contrary and cantankerous characteristics will soon have him tearing his hair out with vigorous vexation. In return, his painstaking and pernickety practices will leave you open-mouthed in amazement, making this a partnership that's over almost before it's begun.

AQUARIUS WOMAN AND LIBRA MAN

The more platonic and easy-going your relationship, the better it'll be. That's what you've got to remember if you want to keep chummy with a chap born under the banner of lovely Libra. You both belong to the Airy section of the celestial set-up, and you'll adore the mental magnetism that brings you two together – after all, neither of you wants a darling who's a dolt or dullard. Emotionally, though, it's quite another story, as you don't like being tied down and the sweet, soft and sensual ways of your Libran lover could soon start to cloy or turn sour. When you're ensconced in the bedroom there may be a few more surprises in store for your unsuspecting Venusian, whether you suggest doing something he doesn't even know about, or announce that you've decided to give up sex for the summer. It'll take a few compromises before you can settle down together, but if anyone can teach a strong-minded Aquarian lass like you the art of give and take, then it's a diplomatic Libran lad!

AQUARIUS WOMAN AND SCORPIO MAN

What a crazy couple! You two many never get further than just being good friends, because you're at opposite ends of the astrological rainbow. For a start, your Scorpio swain is a wee bit traditional and conservative, so your weird and wonderful ways could leave him speechless with shock, surprise and stupefaction. To make it worse, you both belong to Fixed signs, which means that once you've made up your mind about something there's almost nothing on earth that will make you change it. You'll be phenomenally faithful to each other and tremendously trustworthy, but the minute there's a disagreement neither of you will want to back down, admit you're wrong or say you're sorry. Your Scorpio chap is usually the first one to crack – along with the china he'll chuck at you! As for sex, your desires may be so different that you can never get going.

AQUARIUS WOMAN AND SAGITTARIUS MAN

'Guess what?' That's the way you'll start all your conversations when you join forces with a smashing Centaur, because you'll never run out of things to say to each other. You're both full of curiosity about the world and its ways, so you'll be perfect companions whenever you embark on any journeys of the mind or body that take your fancy. As well as the love and laughter between you, you'll also be linked by a strong sense of respect for each other's ideas, thoughts and intelligence. You'll thrill to your Saggy sweetheart's adventurous spirit, and he'll find it hard to hide a smile whenever you say or do something shocking, especially if it's in front of pompous or patronising people. As for your emotions, neither of you enjoys stormy scenes, jealous gibes or intense interludes of steamy sex, so you'll try to keep these things light and bright. Any challenges that arise you'll take in your stride, so you can triumph together. Terrific!

AQUARIUS WOMAN AND CAPRICORN MAN

Before you go any further, are you ruled by unruly Uranus or sturdy Saturn? If you're motivated by that perplexing planet Uranus, then your relationship could be about as exciting as a damp squib, because you just won't understand each other one bit. On the other hand, if you're strongly Saturnine, then you'll be quite Capricorn in character, though you'll still act the Aquarian and take him by surprise sometimes. You'll be as happy as sandboys and sandgirls together, and sexually things will go with a real swing, but if you're truly Uranian then you could both give up in disgust and read a good book instead! You just won't have anything in common, and your Capricorn chap's sober and sensible ways will clash catastrophically with your avant-garde and original approach to life. You could both find it all too difficult to deal with.

AQUARIUS WOMAN AND AQUARIUS MAN

The first thing to fathom out when you two meet is which planets have dominance over your personalities. If it's steadfast Saturn, then you'll both have a strong streak of Capricorn in your characters, but if it's unconventional Uranus then your relationship will be either a sure-fire success or an out-and-out failure. You see, you'll be so similar that you could drive each other completely round the bend! However, if you're excited, exhilarated and entertained by being with someone as cranky and quirky as yourself, then you'll be in clover with an Aquarian *homme*. The way you lead your lives is bound to cause comment from more conservative chums, but that won't matter one jot to you two. Emotionally, your feelings may swing from sexy to stone cold, but it'll all be grist to your magical mill, and you'll love being with a partner who's as independent, inimitable and unique as yourself.

AQUARIUS WOMAN AND PISCES MAN

What's all this about? There could be torrents of tears and stacks of sobs when you meet up with a Piscean chap, and one thing's for sure – it won't be you who's doing the crying! The sexual roles could be completely reversed when you give your love to a Fishy fellow, because he may be much more emotional, sentimental and soft-hearted than you. Things will be a lot easier if you're crammed with Capricornian characteristics, but if you're Uranian through and through this could be a very perplexing pairing indeed. Whenever your Piscean paramour floats off into a fantasy land of his own or does his martyr act that's designed to play on your sympathies (it won't), you'll be itching to give him a good shake, or just let him get on with it. Emotional blackmail leaves you cold, and you're far too concerned with the future to get all worked up about the past. You'll both have to put in a lot of hard work if you want this contrary coupling to continue, but can either of you be bothered?

VENUS AND YOU

The planet of love, beauty, harmony and all things artistic, Venus is a very important influence on our lives indeed. She's considered to be a particularly feminine planet, and is associated with the emotions, money, social life, possessions, partnerships, clothes and fashion.

Folk who have a strong Venus in their solar charts may be anything from stunningly attractive to very beautiful indeed, and they also have refined tastes, are gentle, placid, diplomatic, understanding and creative. On the other hand, people with negative Venusian traits can be lazy, over-indulgent, soppy, too sweet for words or impractical. Luscious Venus also rules the throat, lower back and kidneys, and folk with strong Venusian placings are often blessed with beautiful voices and a deep love or appreciation of music.

LOVING VIBRATIONS

Although Venus rules the signs of Taurus and Libra, nevertheless she also has an important part to play in *everyone*'s natal horoscope, for her placing and aspects will tell an astrologer volumes about a person's love life, artistic attributes, how strong their powers of attraction are and how they relate to others. If you've often wondered why you react amorously in a way that's contrary or contradictory to your Sun sign, it could well be because your

49

natal Venus occupies a different sign, whether it's adjacent to your own or two signs away from your Sun sign.

Well, whether you know the position of Venus in your own natal chart or not, following her progress through the starry skies in the coming year will still give you a helping hand where all loving liaisons and artistic affairs are concerned. Follow my instructions here and you'll be able to plot the course of sweet Venus as she progresses through your horoscope.

The zodiac consists of twelve houses, each ruled by a particular Sun sign. When velvety Venus occupies your Sun sign, she's said to be in your first solar house, and when she moves on to the next sign she occupies your second solar house, and so on, until she's travelled right around the zodiac.

THE EFFECTS OF VENUS

Each time she changes houses and signs, she influences a different part of your life. For example, whenever she visits your Sun sign (your first solar abode), she makes you even more delectable, dazzling, debonair and delightful than usual. When she glides through a sign that's compatible with yours (and that means your third, fifth, ninth and eleventh houses), you feel full of the joys of spring, happy and harmonious, but when she traverses signs that aren't amenable to yours (in other words, your fourth, seventh and tenth houses), your loving feelings can take a slightly tricky turn, or you may even be too indulgent for your own good.

VENUS IN YOUR HOROSCOPE

So, if you want to keep track of your loving feelings, and follow voluptuous Venus' sojourn around the celestial skies, all you have to do is fill in the blank zodiac wheel and then refer to The Progress of Venus in 1990, showing her movements every month. For instance, if you're a sun sign Capricorn and it's 9th June, then look at the tables for that month. They'll tell you that Venus entered Taurus on 30th May and will stay there until 25th June, so if you consult your own Zodiac wheel you'll see that she's in your fifth solar abode during that time, so read Venus in your Fifth house. Easy isn't it?

VENUS POSITIONS IN 1990

Begins the year in Aquarius

January 16th	15.24	into Capricorn (moving retrograde)
March 3rd	17.53	into Aquarius (moving direct again)
April 6th	9.14	into Pisces
May 4th	3.53	into Aries
May 30th	10.14	into Taurus
June 25th	0.15	into Gemini
July 20th	3.42	into Cancer
August 13th	22.06	into Leo
September 7th	8.22	into Virgo
October 1st	12.14	into Libra
October 25th	12.04	into Scorpio
November 18th	9.59	into Sagittarius
December 12th	7.19	into Capricorn

VENUS IN YOUR FIRST HOUSE

If you've got it, then flaunt it! (And if you haven't, then pretend that you have!) Those are the mottoes to remember at the moment, for it's a terrific time to cash in on your innate charm and captivating charisma, and entrance everyone around you! Even if you'll never win a beauty contest, you should make a sterling effort now to bring out your best assets and attributes. Want to win someone round to your side, turn the head of a prospective partner or just knock everyone dead with your wonderful ways? Then pull out all the stops and you'll be amazed at what you can do! Primping, preening, prettifying and generally gilding the lily that is you are all activities that will appeal now. Splash out on potions, powders and perfumes, a smashing new outfit or a different but dazzling hairdo. You can make great strides ahead now by emphasising your personality and appearance, so don't be backwards in coming forwards!

VENUS IN YOUR SECOND HOUSE

A thing of beauty is a joy forever! That's how you feel at the moment, making you long to be surrounded by pretty possessions,

51

VENUS AND YOU

This chart shows the astrological houses which have been numbered for someone born with the Sun in Capricorn

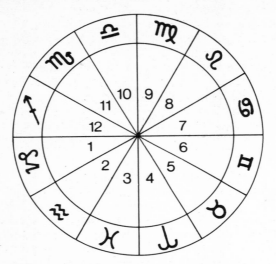

This is a blank chart ready for you to fill in. Start off by writing the number one by your Sun sign, then continue around the wheel in an anti-clockwise direction until you have reached number twelve

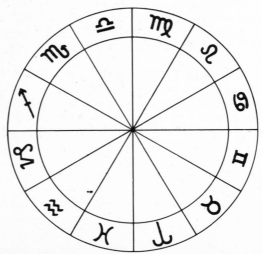

arty antiques and little luxuries that bring you happiness and harmony. If you don't already own them then you'll be scampering off to the shops before you can say 'I'll take it'! Quality, not quantity, is what you're after now, so you're likely to head for Harrods and cop out of the Co-op, or go for the most gorgeous grub and grog you can find! Unless your taste is always top notch then you may need to be careful now, for although you *could* show a superb artistic appreciation, on the other hand once Venus has moved on you may find that you've gone for things that are gaudy and garish. Whoops! Folks love having you around now, so if you want to earn some pin money speak up whilst others are amenable. Better watch your spending though, or that cash will disappear at the speed of light!

VENUS IN YOUR THIRD HOUSE

Personality plus! That's you at the moment, making you a grand person to have around and high on everyone's list of favourite folk. It's your congenial, convivial and captivating ways that are attracting all the amiable attention, but you'll soon fall from grace if you grow a swollen head or become too conceited for words, so watch out! You could become very embroiled and involved in community concerns and local matters now, filling you with fond feelings for your surroundings and making you long for them to be as pretty and personable as possible. If you're looking for love then you could find it's been on your doorstep all the time, when you fall for a neighbour or even a cousin, or you could be introduced to someone special in a superficial setting by a sibling! It's also a grand opportunity to show the folk you see everyday just how much they really do mean to you – come on, don't be shy!

VENUS IN YOUR FOURTH HOUSE

Home is where your heart is whilst cosy Venus traverses through your fourth solar abode, filling you with an overpowering need to be amongst you and yours and know that you're loved, adored and appreciated. Playing happy families with kith and kin will warm the cockles of your heart, and if you've had a contretemps with one of the clan then this is your chance to forgive and forget. Is your domestic domain looking dreary and drab? Then get out the paints and papers and turn it into somewhere sumptuous 'cos you're in the mood for rich fabrics, comfy furniture and anything with 'olde worlde' charm right now. Just make sure you don't spend, spend, spend! Golden memories and treasured keepsakes that remind you of the good old days are also dear to your heart at the moment. Don't stay at home all the time, as a relative or friend of the family could introduce you to someone very special indeed . . .

VENUS IN YOUR FIFTH HOUSE

Delightful, delicious, delectable and de-lovely! Love is everywhere, so make the very most of this pleasurable patch! In fact, you're surrounded by an auspicious aura of amour and affection, helping you to get on with everyone you meet. Affairs *de coeur* are starred for success, and whether you've been together for more years than you care to remember or are just starting a smashing starry-eyed romance, you'll wear your heart on your sleeve. You may also meet the man or maiden of your dreams, but beware of reading more into a situation than really exists or falling in love with love. Remember that love comes in many forms, and an artistic endeavour, creative concern, cuddly pet or wee child may provide all you need in the way of enrichment, happiness and satisfaction. One word of warning – your willpower's at an all-time low and you'll indulge yourself in all sorts of enjoyable ways, but know when pleasure stops and work starts.

VENUS IN YOUR SIXTH HOUSE

Whistle while you work! Whatever you do in your workaday world, you'll really enjoy yourself now. What's more, your working conditions will be more convivial and conducive at the moment, especially if you add tiny touches of your own with flowers, potted plants or even some of your favourite knick-knacks to brighten the place up. If you've fallen out with a client or colleague, then pour oil on troubled waters now, and if someone new has joined your firm or factory make 'em feel welcome and at home. Who knows, it could even turn into something special and be the start of anything from a firm friendship to a ravishing romance! Works outings, office parties and wassails with your workmates will all be especially enjoyable, so throw yourself into the fun. If you went overboard when voluptuous Venus was in your fifth solar abode, then you may pay for all that indulgence now. Better exercise your way back to peak condition!

VENUS IN YOUR SEVENTH HOUSE
Are those wedding bells I hear? Partnerships of all persuasions are looking luscious at the moment, and if you've been a single soul then this could be when you become one half of a contented couple, whether professional, platonic or provocatively passionate! What a time for making whoopee! One thing's for sure, you need the comfort of companionship and the reassurance of knowing that you're loved and cared for now, whether that's through wooing words, ardent actions or devoted deeds, but don't forget that dear ones will also like to know how you feel about *them*! It's much easier than normal to tune into the way folk feel about you, and they'll adore your empathy and sympathy for their loving feelings. In fact, everyone will be happy! It's a terrific time for plighting your troth or declaring undying love, and even if you're more like Darby and Joan your relationship will be like a second honeymoon.

VENUS IN YOUR EIGHTH HOUSE
Pungent passions, fervent feelings and exotic emotions are on your amorous agenda at the moment, imbuing all encounters and intimate affairs with increased intensity and a stronger significance than usual. What's more, your libido's on the rise, making you long to increase your passion ration and let loose all your lusty, sensual and erotic urges and surges. Talk about hot stuff – you're burning with desire now, and could fall head over heels in lust with a very sexy and salacious soul indeed! It's a torrid time, but don't let your partner think that you're only interested in their body and not their brain, or be tempted to trade off your sexual favours for mercenary or materialistic motives. Something else to watch is a possible predilection for power, making you enjoy organising folk around you or calling all the shots. You may also go on a spending spree – but with your other half's cash, so tread carefully!

VENUS IN YOUR NINTH HOUSE
Super duper! It's your love for the world around you that's being awakened now, broadening your mental and physical horizons and encouraging you to explore the serious and spiritual side of life. Travelling to far-away places will be ultra-enjoyable now, and you might even have a holiday romance that truly puts the

cheery cherry on your cosmopolitan cake! Even if you stay put you could fall for someone from another clime, creed or culture, or even marry one who takes you away from the country of your birth. There's definitely an international flavour in the air that'll spice up all your dealings now. Developments in a loving liaison could increase your insight and understanding of your relationship, or an amour may introduce you to a fascinating new side of life. Want to increase your brain power? Then sign up for an evening class or further education course – who knows who you may meet along the way . . . ?

VENUS IN YOUR TENTH HOUSE
Vocational Venus! People in power and influential folk are smiling favourably at the moment, so cash in on your attributes! Not only will you get on better with parents, senior citizens and father figures, but any dealings with managers, magnates or moguls will also go well. Play your cards right and success could be yours due to the strength of your personality, smart appearance or artistic gifts. If love enters your life now you may fall for someone who comes from a different social strata or is way above you in other areas. Watch out for amour with ambitious or opportunist overtones, for that might make you set your cap at a boss, bigwig or someone who's loaded with loot, just for what you can get out of the liaison. Even if you're not aware of your mercenary machinations, they could ruin the relationship once they're revealed. It's a grand time to mix business with pleasure, and win others round to your ideas.

VENUS IN YOUR ELEVENTH HOUSE
Friendship, friendship, that's the perfect friendship, so don't keep yourself to yourself! Gregarious gatherings, social scenarios, group get-togethers and neighbourly natterings will all be highly enjoyable, as well as an introduction to all sorts of fresh and fascinating folk. If you've just moved to pastures new and are felling left out or lonely, then start chatting to the people next door, join a club or social group or find a hobby that'll be your passport to meeting personable people. Not only may you make some mates, but you might even meet that special someone you've been searching for all life long! Been cherishing a particular hope or dream? Then you'll adore throwing yourself into the swing of

things now, so you can get your plans and projects off the ground and into action. A revelation could also come your way now when you realise that a person who's been a pal is also the love of your life – what a turn up for the books!

VENUS IN YOUR TWELFTH HOUSE

A radiant ring of ravishing romance surrounds you now, endowing all your emotions with a very nebulous, nectarine and even naive flavour. Amour may take a very spiritual and selfless turn when you have to give up something important for a loved one, or devote yourself to looking after someone who'll depend on you body and soul. Even so, make sure you're acting from the best of motives, and don't confuse self-sacrifice with acting the put-upon martyr! Charitable or voluntary ventures, and dealings with institutions, hospitals, prisons and the like could also be to the fore now. A love affair starting now has all the makings of a fairy tale, but don't read more into it than really exists or think that you've kissed a prince or princess – only to see them turn back into a frog! Self-deception may be rife now. You could also begin an affair and have to keep things very hush-hush indeed – you'll love every minute of it!

THE TRADITIONS OF ASTROLOGY

SIGN	NOs	COLOUR	DAY	STONE	METAL	FLOWER	BODY AREA
Aries	1	Red	Tuesday	Diamond	Iron	Geranium	Head
Taurus	2	Copper, dark blue	Friday	Emerald	Copper	Daisy	Throat
Gemini	3	Yellows	Wednesday	Agate, garnet	Mercury	Daffodil	Hands, chest
Cancer	4	Pearl, silver	Monday	Pearl	Silver	White rose, lily	Breast
Leo	5	Amber, gold	Sunday	Ruby	Gold	Sunflower	Heart, spine
Virgo	6	Autumnal shades	Wednesday	Peridot	Mercury	Lily of the valley	Intestines
Libra	7	Pastel blues and pinks	Friday	Sapphire	Copper	Rose	Kidneys
Scorpio	8	Black, burgundy	Tuesday	Opal	Iron	Dahlia, rhododendron	Sexual organs
Sagittarius	9	Imperial purple	Thursday	Topaz	Tin	Delphinium	Thighs, hips
Capricorn	10, 1	Black, grey, white	Saturday	Turquoise	Lead	Pansy	Shins, knees
Aquarius	11, 2	Turquoise, blues	Saturday	Amethyst	Lead	Crocus, snowdrop	Ankles
Pisces	12, 3	Greens, sea blues	Thursday	Aquamarine	Tin	Poppy	Feet

WHAT 1990 HAS IN STORE
FOR YOUR
LOVE, CASH AND WORK

LOVE

Sensitive, sublime Aquarius. That's you in humanitarian 1990. You have all sorts of sympathetic feelings for the plight of others that surface from time to time, making you want to shoulder the world's responsibilities all on your own. Of course you can't, but you may sometimes get involved in causes and charities where at least you can do something to help. This year your humanitarian streak is strong, too, and there's a good chance you'll meet someone of like mind, especially in the last quarter of 1990 when Jupiter enters your solar houses of love and relationship. You could be swept off your feet and fall hook, line and sinker for somebody then. Or if you're already one half of a happy twosome you'll see a strengthening and bonding in your relationship that brings bliss and happiness into your world in new and exciting ways. But other partnerships are star-studded too, and if you're planning to join an organisation, humanitarian or connected with charity in some way, then you'll get that deep feeling of satisfaction that comes when you know you've done something really worthwhile for your fellow man.

CASH

Lots of lolly isn't important for you this humanitarian annum. You won't have any pecuniary problems worth speaking about and you're too busy climbing to dizzier and dizzier heights career-wise to worry about the bank balance, which is taking care of itself quite nicely anyway. Of course, all your extra efforts this year will bring in plenty of extra cash, but honour, prestige and personal dignity are what you're about now. The boodle comes and the boodle goes. When you're broke you don't care, and when you've got plenty of pounds in your pocket, well, its only money isn't it? That's your attitude to money – it comes second place to the more important things in life. You're not going to lose any sleep over it, you can leave that to your bank manager, can't you? What a refreshing attitude to finance, if only the rest of the world were like that. Some folk might think you're irresponsible, but in their heart of hearts they know you're right. Don't change, Aquarius!

WORK

Goodness! What amazing, astounding opportunities await you this year, Aquarius? The sky's the limit career- and work-wise. You'll be busy doing all sorts of new and exciting things, expanding your horizons and diversifying your talents. Whole new work experiences will open up before you. Expansive Jupiter is passing through your solar houses of work and health until mid-August; coupled with powerful Pluto transforming your prospects and adding to your personal esteem you could be very much in the public image in your career. You won't mind being showered with recognition and honours, will you? After all, you know you deserve it. But busy as you'll be, 1990 will also set you thinking about the direction of your career, just where you'll be going from now on. You'll throw out all those avenues that are no longer useful or productive and start turning in new, more useful and sometimes completely different directions. Charting uncharted waters won't be a problem for you. Your insight and skill will take you right to the heart of things, and nobody likes the new and unusual more than you, Aquarius.

YOUR DAY-BY-DAY GUIDE TO 1990

JANUARY

MONDAY, 1st. Monetary matters are not necessarily your favourite topic, but as you put your best foot forward into this brave new decade you can't help realising that a creative way with cash could be the cornerstone of the success of your hopes and wishes. Economic inspiration is apt to strike you from the most surprising sources, so don't restrict yourself to the tried and trusted ways of managing your material resources when there are more modern methods that will suit your purposes.

TUESDAY, 2nd. Utterly mystical, magical and mysterious, that's you this Tuesday as the Sun mingles his mighty powers with those of Neptune, the lord of the dream world. Don't plan to tackle anything too practical today, for you're so supremely sensitive to the subtleties of life your talents are much better used in an effort to understand the hidden meanings and motivations of yourself and the folk around you. Quiet contemplation of your unconscious impulses will reveal much to you now.

WEDNESDAY, 3rd. Mentally you're mesmerised by an unexpected idea that swamps your mind with striking images and fantastic notions. At first sight your notions all seem quite sensible, but don't let that fool you into taking them too seriously, for a close examination will reveal fatal flaws in your logic and reasoning. Don't start blabbing about your brilliant concepts until you've worked out a few of the down to earth details.

THURSDAY, 4th. By way of complete contrast, Madam Moon is gripped by Saturn's icy rays today, putting a very chilly and cheerless face forward. It seems there's a little barrier of silence around you as people you thought were warm and affectionate turn their backs on you and manage to misunderstand every word you utter. Keep your head down and concentrate on mundane matters for this dejected day will quickly pass.

FRIDAY, 5th. With so many important planets in your solar house of the unconscious it is no wonder you've been having a few funny turns and peculiar notions lately. This is one of those days when you'll be able to tune in to an intuitive insight in your own inner incentives and unconscious motivations. Psychic abilities are stirring beneath the surface of your mind, so even if it strikes you as nonsensical you should investigate the subject impartially.

SATURDAY, 6th. It's beginning to dawn on you that fine notions and fancy dreams may not be enough on their own to help you achieve all you're aiming for in the 1990s, for there are certain puzzling practicalities to be sorted out before you can attain an ideal world for all and sundry. It is all very tiresome, for you'd much rather live in a delicious dream world than tackle the pragmatic problems involved in life, but there's no point in trying to escape reality now.

SUNDAY, 7th. Sit back and ponder your most ambitious plans – is your current strategy working well? Or are there hidden flaws that need to be attended to before they turn into major failings? You're a terrific tactician these days, so whilst you're sitting back after your Sunday lunch think through your business techniques and see if you can come up with a more subtle and perceptive plan to succeed in your aims.

MONDAY, 8th. A fervent friend with a bee in their bonnet will sting you into irritated action today, but instead of jumping joyfully on the bandwagon they're promoting you are more likely to run a mile just to escape their high-powered pressure. Don't reject a cause that could mean a great deal to you simply because it's presented in an insensitive way, as once you've overcome your initial reaction you may find there is much to be recommended in the basic concept.

TUESDAY, 9th. Anyone who tried to pull the wool over your eyes this Tuesday will very quickly discover the error of their ways, as you see instantly through the most subtle stratagem, almost as though you had X-ray eyes! Turn your incredibly intuitive mind to the problems involved in a charitable effort you're interested in, for it's in helping others you're at your most astute and intelligent now. What an ingenious Aquarian you are!

WEDNESDAY, 10th. One of the few failings associated with an Aquarian nature can be a trifling tendency to be a paragon of perfection. Your high personal standards set an excellent example to us all, but there are times when you're inclined to be a little too strict, severe and stern with us lesser mortals as well as with yourself. Be a little more forgiving and flexible and you'll find life much easier!

THURSDAY, 11th. Look carefully at what you are getting from your current occupation, for if it appears to be leading into an employment dead-end now is your chance to make a move designed to launch you back into the mainstream. Out of work Water-carriers will find that the tide's about to turn, but you may have to make an irrevocable decision requiring a momentous move and major alteration in your ambitions first.

FRIDAY, 12th. The cold winds may blow, but that doesn't bother you and the love of your life, for there's a fervent flame of love burning in the hearth of your hearts, keeping you both as warm as toast! Romantically this is a ravishingly rapturous day, so if you're still seeking your soul mate now's your chance to look around with a love-light in your eye. Togetherness tops your astral agenda this Friday.

SATURDAY, 13th. Your other half is normally so sane and sensible, but for once I wouldn't advise you to take everything they say at face value for they could be playing a devious and deceitful game with your emotions today. It's up to you to figure out precisely what has triggered this outburst of spite, but if I were you I'd look in the area of professional jealousy and envy of your worldly successes. Maybe all they want is to share in your achievements?

SUNDAY, 14th. The hidden world of the psychic, supernatural and spiritual side of life is absolutely fascinating to you these days and on Sunday you're especially attuned to your own inner thoughts, feelings and insights on the topic. This is a brilliant opportunity to mount a delicate investigation into any personal puzzles and perplexities rooted in your unconscious assumptions and ideals, as you'll understand your irrational and illogical impulses with ease and will know how to make the most of your instinctive abilities. Practicalities must take a back seat now.

MONDAY, 15th. Even the most independent Aquarian must take others into account from time to time when dealing with some large-scale legal or financial affairs, even if it's just working with your accountant to keep the taxman happy. For once you've the patience required to plough through the paperwork involved in setting your affairs on a firm and economically secure foundation so seize the opportunity to chat with an expert or seek out an adviser who will help you make the most of your resources.

TUESDAY, 16th. Professionally this entire period is a time of profound transformation in your life as you reassess the fundamental design and direction of your career plans. You can no longer ignore your spiritual needs in the interest of making a big splash socially or vocationally. Think through your overall aims and aspirations in life from very first principles and strip away any superfluous or unimportant ambitions. Major changes can easily be made now that would be very difficult at any other time.

WEDNESDAY, 17th. You're certainly living up to your rebellious reputation today, as all sorts of weird and wonderful notions pop unannounced into your head and set you off on a mental wild-goose chase. You're completely wrapped up in an imaginative and intuitive world of your own, which is utterly enthralling to you but a mite mystifying to anyone not on your wave-length. Don't get too impatient if folk don't know what you're on about, as we can't all be geniuses!

THURSDAY, 18th. Who would have thought you'd have such a soft-hearted, sympathetic and downright sentimental side? It may make you blush to admit it, but an emotionally weighted appeal to your better nature from someone in need will melt your heart instantly and make you bend over backwards to help anyone who tugs at your heart-strings. I won't tell anyone if you want to keep up your cool, calm and collected image, but we both know your compassionate secret.

FRIDAY, 19th. A tiny clue that you pick up on almost by accident today could alert you to the fact that there are people in a position of power who are far from being the competent and capable professionals they claim. There's not much in the way of clear evidence to support any open accusations, but don't ignore your hunch just yet. By investigating more closely and trusting to your own intuition you could uncover some sensitive secrets that need to be aired more openly.

SATURDAY, 20th. All systems go! That's the celestial message for you this super Saturday for the splendid rays of the Sun move majestically into your own sign and imbue you with creative and expressive skills that will dazzle one and all in the coming weeks. It's time you came out of the closet and broadcast your own special talents far and wide as you're at your impressive and spirited best.

SUNDAY, 21st. Now you're in such fine fettle, oozing energy and enthusiasm, you're keen to congregate with a crowd of cheerful chums so why not arrange for a wee get-together in your own home? By turning your abode into a meeting-place for your friends you'll assure yourself an interesting and enjoyable time at the centre of a stimulating social scene. What a popular soul you are!

MONDAY, 22nd. You're still swept away on a wave of sociable impulses and invitations so don't be put off your affable stroke by the fact that it's a mundane Monday. On a more serious level you're instinctively aware of the need to care for the less fortunate members of the family of mankind and will want to join in with a movement designed to help the underprivileged. Even if all you can manage is a modest donation to a worthy cause, it'll make you feel better.

TUESDAY, 23rd. Theoretically you love the idea that the whole world is one big happy family, but there are some people who make it very difficult to accept in practice! You're inclined to run a mile from comrades and companions who try to pin you down to a positive commitment on this temperamental Tuesday, for even though your ideals are very alike you refuse to be pigeon-holed and placed in a common category. Social gatherings get on your nerves today.

WEDNESDAY, 24th. There are some very sensitive and delicate situations to be dealt with in your world this Wednesday, from helping a pal who's poorly to applying your spiritual ideals to a practical problem. You don't mean to be unkind, but your patience is wearing very thin with the constant demands for you to submerge your own personal interests for the good of others. You'll have to stand up for yourself at some point, for you're just not suited to playing the role of martyr.

THURSDAY, 25th. Anyone who tries to get through to you today would be forced to conclude that you really are as cool as a cucumber and may decide that's the way you like it, but in fact you hate feeling so emotionally cut off from the people around you. Your confident appearance is often just a front for an intricate complex of fears, doubts and misgivings about your own abilities. Don't take your inner anxieties too seriously for they will soon pass.

FRIDAY, 26th. With the powerful presence of today's solar eclipse in your own sign you're in an unusually emotional state, fully in touch with feelings you've been ignoring and overlooking for some time. Follow a hunch concerning a personal path that's beginning to appear in front of you, as this is the perfect time to make a fresh beginning, whether that means updating your appearance or rearranging your lifestyle to reflect your aims and ambitions in this brand new decade.

SATURDAY, 27th. Mini Mercury's ensnared once more in Neptune's nebulous net, and as a result your mind is flooded with fantastic images and noble notions. It may seem as clear as day that you should devote yourself to a selfless cause, but don't be committed long-term until you've thought things through in the clear light of day for you're inclined to be far too trusting. There are unscrupulous folk about ready to take full advantage of your gullible idealism.

SUNDAY, 28th. You've put in more than your fair share of work and worry this week and it's high time you refreshed your stressed spirit with a dip into the pool of pleasure provided by your personal pals. All it takes is a few moments' chat to fill you with the joys of life once more, so even if it's just a few words over the garden fence with your neighbour, make sure you make contact with some friendly folk this Sunday.

MONDAY, 29th. To all intents and purposes you're entering a placid and passive phase as macho Mars disappears from sight in your solar house of secrets. That is not quite true, for there is plenty of feverish and frenzied activity taking place in your inner world as you struggle to find a way of combining selfless spiritual ideals with your egotistical desires. For a while you may have to sacrifice your own wishes in order to serve others, so accept your fate cheerfully rather than ranting and raving against it.

TUESDAY, 30th. A message reaches you today that highlights the battle being fought in your heart and head, for your ego demands a certain reaction whilst your own ideals insist on a more sensitive and sympathetic response. You'll need to wrestle with your conscience for a wee while, but really you know what you must do. You don't like putting your own interests behind your principles though, and it'll put you in quite a mood all day.

WEDNESDAY, 31st. You're tempted to try and explain your reasons to someone who questions your recent actions, for you hate to feel misunderstood or misrepresented. Don't be surprised if all you succeed in doing is to add to the cloud of confusion surrounding you as you're not at your most rational and reasonable just now. Psychic or supernatural interests appear fascinating, but may not be as enlightening as you think.

FEBRUARY

THURSDAY, 1st. As far as you're concerned there's no earthly reason why you shouldn't have the best of both worlds and proceed to an elevated level in your field of employment without sacrificing any of your spare-time interests and altruistic activities. I hate to disillusion you, but the chances are you'll stretch far beyond your own capabilities if you don't take a more modest view of your aptitudes and abilities. Unemployed Water-carriers have a good chance of impressing the powers that be through a sensitive and compassionate approach.

FRIDAY, 2nd. You're such a free and independent spirit you're not normally to be found lapping up the cosy and comforting luxuries of home, but this Friday you're in the mood to be cosseted and coddled a little. In fact, before you feel you can fully face up to the challenge of this demanding new decade you should take a bit of a stroll down memory lane. Nostalgia may be going out of style, but it'll refresh your spirits no end!

SATURDAY, 3rd. In the wonderful world of your imagination it's such a simple matter to bring about a world run on kind, compassionate and totally sympathetic lines, but in the real world there are endless complications to be taken into account. You've been trying to ignore this uncomfortable fact for too long, and now you're being forced to take the practicalities more seriously. Don't jump to the conclusion that your dreams are about to vanish in the cold light of day, for with patient persistence much can be achieved.

SUNDAY, 4th. If there are youngsters in your world who have been neglected lately this is a fine time to play a few games and generally renew your acquaintance with them, as they'll be thrilled at being the centre of attention for a while. You also have a very welcome opportunity today to spend some time on a pet pastime or project, as you're creatively in an intuitive and inspired state.

MONDAY, 5th. Are you sure you haven't been taking elocution or public speaking lessons? Either that or your innate eloquence is showing through, for you have wonderfully winning words today, whether you're whispering sweet nothings to the love of your life or putting forward a professional proposal to someone you hope will help you. Use your persuasive powers to promote peace in all areas of your personal world, for now no one can resist your seductive speech!

TUESDAY, 6th. You're inclined to be a wee bit intransigent when you feel there's an important issue at stake, but you may find yourself in hot water today if you dig in your toes a little too stubbornly. You can't underestimate the power of some autocratic authorities to make life difficult for you, so however much you hate playing their devious and deceitful games you mustn't call their bluff until you are quite sure you're strong enough to beat them on their own territory. You could be your own worst enemy today.

WEDNESDAY, 7th. Before you start crying on my shoulder and complaining that your partner in life just doesn't understand you perhaps you'd better pause and ponder the fact that it takes two to tango. There's a barrier between you and the people you care most about as solid as a brick wall, but it'll take more than self-pity and regret to set matters right again. Don't wait for your other half to make the first move.

THURSDAY, 8th. Your affairs of the heart have been going through a mighty peculiar and puzzling patch lately so you'll be relieved to hear that Venus the seductress has taken pity on you and will be standing by to help you unravel the tangled romantic threads from this Thursday. It may take some time until you and your loved one are out of the woods, but at least you can look forward to a more open and uncomplicated amour.

FRIDAY, 9th. Friday's Full Moon in your opposite sign of Leo signals the fact that this is a crucial time for partnerships of all descriptions. If there are certain issues you've swept under the carpet or problems you hoped would disappear in time you must face up to facts now. If you've been drifting apart it may be time to make the break, but if there's life in your relationship yet you should eliminate areas of annoyance at once. An impetuous impulse to break free whatever the cost is unlikely to be in your best interests.

SATURDAY, 10th. If your 'New Decade' resolutions are beginning to fall by the wayside, especially where your health and physical fitness are concerned, don't simply give up and assume they are a lost cause, for by taking yourself in hand now you can get right back into the swing of things. Maybe you'd do better with a friend or associate to keep you company as you exercise or otherwise look after yourself? Confide in someone you trust implicitly and they'll be happy to help.

SUNDAY, 11th. You're such a unique, inventive and original individual! Brilliant brainwaves bubble up from your imagination almost without effort this Sunday, filling you with hope for the fate of your personal projects. If you're canny you'll keep quiet about the full potential of your ideas, as by exploiting them in secret for a wee while you'll reap much richer rewards from your own efforts, and that's only fair. Don't let fraudulent folk take unfair advantage of your resourceful skills.

MONDAY, 12th. The heavens' wandering wayfarer seeks your hospitality from Monday so be prepared for an interesting few weeks as the host of madcap Mercury! You're in a loquacious league of your own when it comes to getting your ideas across and generally persuading people to back your projects. This is a splendid time to organise short journeys and local appointments as you'll knock spots off any competition.

TUESDAY, 13th. A restless, reckless and restive mood has you in its grip today and as a result you're like a cat on a hot tin roof. Your daily routine had better be pretty varied if you're to avoid getting on everyone's nerves as well as your own, so if possible plan a day that will get you out and about rather than keep you tied to your desk or the kitchen sink. If that's out of the question, dive into the domain of your own dreams and leave the tedious and tiresome details of life to another day.

WEDNESDAY, 14th. They say this is a day for romance, but you're not about to fall for any old flannel that comes your way. You've nothing against amour and will be happy to make sure your other half knows how much you care, but you're not at all keen on taking things any further than that. You tend to smell a trap when people protest too much about their passionate adoration and feel uncomfortable with lavish declarations of undying love. On the whole, you'll be quite pleased when all the fuss is over!

THURSDAY, 15th. You're not usually bashful, but you have a chance on Thursday to talk to someone in a position of authority in your profession, and the prospect is a bit alarming. So long as you stick to the point and don't let your heart overrule your head on any of the subjects you cover you'll be fine. Jobless Aquarians may find an appeal to the feelings of folk in power will help to swing an important decision their way.

FRIDAY, 16th. The full blaze of the heavenly spotlight turns on your horoscopic house of careers, ambitions and worldly aspirations today, forcing you to accept a few home truths about your professional position. By being totally honest with yourself about your own ambitions and abilities you can devise a plan of action that will propel you powerfully into a position of much greater prominence and prestige.

SATURDAY, 17th. There's treachery afoot in the heavens and in your own world as well, but just where the problem is liable to come from I really wouldn't like to say. You'll need to be on your guard against almost everyone until you've figured out who's likely to betray you or undermine your effectiveness. If there are decisions to be made or documents to sign you should wait for another day, for mistakes made now could be costly and complicated.

SUNDAY, 18th. You've had your fair share of financial problems in the past, but from Sunday the all-powerful Sun ushers in a period of much greater prosperity. Your personal wealth and sense of worth can be strengthened enormously in the coming month if you put your mind to sorting out a better organised budget or putting in for some extra income. Your earning capacity is on the up-and-up Aquarius!

MONDAY, 19th. I told you your fiscal stars were shining with a lucid and luxurious light, and Monday may bring welcome news that your cash reserves are to be immediately boosted. It may mean finally landing the job of your dreams with a stupendous salary to match or convincing your present employer that you're worth a handsome raise. Don't hesitate to discuss money matters with one and all, for you're sure to hear information that could prove profitable.

TUESDAY, 20th. There's so much positive promise in your employment world these days you hate to turn down any opportunity to advance your occupational ambitions, but even an unrestricted Aquarian has to draw the line somewhere. The problem is that you're beginning to take your enormous physical vitality for granted. I don't care if you're as strong as Rambo, you can't carry on without an adequate amount of rest and relaxation. You'll wind up a workaholic if you're not careful!

WEDNESDAY, 21st. Domestically your life is running far from smoothly at the moment and on Wednesday you're more than usually alert to signs of emotional upset amongst your nearest and dearest. It tears you apart to have your loved ones at each others' throats, but your attempts at diplomacy are inclined to make matters worse rather than better. Don't make a mountain out of a molehill, for the odd outbreak of bad temper can be found in the best of families!

THURSDAY, 22nd. Psychologically you're a complex wee soul so I won't pretend to know what's going on inside your head, but it's clear to me that there are unnecessary anxieties putting their pressure on you and casting a gloomy shadow around you. We all have problems, but you're beginning to blow them up out of all proportion simply because you're being far too hard on yourself. You're such a perfectionist you find it difficult to forgive the slightest slip, but you must learn to be kinder to yourself.

FRIDAY, 23rd. You've made some pretty perceptive observations on the ways of the world over the last few years, and now you've devised a devious plan to take advantage of your insights. The time has come to act in order to achieve some of your most heartfelt ambitions, but that doesn't mean you should reveal your whole hand to the eyes of the world. Maintain a mysterious profile, whether you're standing for office, going for an eminent job or putting your foot on the first rung of the ladder of success, and you'll arouse much useful interest.

SATURDAY, 24th. There are plenty of power-mad people in this world, wanting to seize control over one and all, and you seem to have run into them all at once this Saturday! It's not because fate is being bloody-minded, but rather because of your own exalted ambitions which tend to come into conflict with the equally elevated aims of others. When you take on a grandiose aim you must expect a certain amount of opposition, but take care that you're not dragged down by the in-fighting to compromise your own principles.

SUNDAY, 25th. With the end of the financial year approaching it's time you got your account books in order and worked out your fiscal strategy in detail for the coming economic annum. There's a New Moon today auguring a more realistic era when it comes to monetary matters so don't simply follow in the pecuniary pattern of the past when by thinking things out anew you could break free of old restrictions and outdated obstacles.

MONDAY, 26th. You're given a golden opportunity this Monday to set foot on the stairway to supreme success in your worldly aims and ambitions, as the go-ahead sky urges you to go for your goals! By investing all your energy, ingenuity and economic strengths into your aims and ambitions you can hardly fail to make an impressive impact in your chosen field. You're an up and coming Aquarian!

TUESDAY, 27th. Like the rest of us you always welcome a chance to make a quick buck, but never at the expense of your own sense of integrity and personal principles. At first sight it may seem as though you must sacrifice your economic interests in order to live up to your ideals, but once you come out in support of your moral, ethical and spiritual stance you'll discover material benefits accrue to you from the most unexpected sources.

WEDNESDAY, 28th. What a wan, weary and worn out Water-carrier! You feel as though the weight of the world is on your shoulders as you take on responsibilities and obligations. Do not burden yourself with tasks you don't really want to do simply out of a sense of guilt, for you won't help anyone by acting the martyr. You must learn to say 'No' when folk start to take your good nature for granted. A difficult and discouraging day.

MARCH

THURSDAY, 1st. A family member may throw a spanner in the works this Thursday and upset some of your carefully laid plans at a moment's notice, but there's no need to kick up a fuss for the resulting upheaval promises to be really quite enjoyable. It will also bring you closer together with your kith and kin. An intuitive hunch about some proposed changes to your abode should be followed up for it will help you make the most of your resources and options.

FRIDAY, 2nd. If you're up against a belligerent boss, bigwig or bureaucrat today you won't get much in the way of sympathy or support from your nearest and dearest, for they're not willing to get too involved in something that is strictly between you and the powers that be. Don't take up an entrenched position, however unfairly it seems you're being treated, for only by cooperating and collaborating will you resolve your stalemate.

SATURDAY, 3rd. Instead of scratching your head over the bills, balances and bank statements littering your desk or mantelpiece, from this Saturday you should knuckle down to the task of organising your affairs more effectively. Mastermind Mercury's helping you think things through, and economic advisers could be just as useful. At the same time, you're entering a period when you ooze attractive appeal from every alluring pore, so don't be surprised if you have to fend off a flock of ardent admirers!

SUNDAY, 4th. I don't usually advise people to think much about work on their day of rest, but for you I'll make an exception as this Sunday's superb stars offer every inducement to thinking out a positive plan of action employment-wise. It may even be worth contacting a few colleagues to discuss your ideas, for they'll appreciate the fact that you have consulted them and may also put you on the trail of a new job or much more lucrative contract. Look at your long-term plans and make sure they're pointing in the right direction!

MONDAY, 5th. The strategy you devised in the peace and quiet of your own home yesterday can be confidently put into action now, as the heavens hold a very optimistic air of forward-looking progress for all Aquarians. An employment opening that's just what you've been seeking is on the cards, especially if you listen to the excellent advice of a more experienced workmate. Your health is blossoming and blooming under the influence of so much enthusiasm!

TUESDAY, 6th. During this stop-start season you mustn't be too downhearted if things don't always go your way. There's a minor setback indicated in today's stars regarding your vocational ambitions, partly owing to the fact that you've overreached yourself and need to consolidate your present position before you forge ahead opening up new ground. Look on the bright side and you'll soon find yourself basking in the sunshine of success!

WEDNESDAY, 7th. You mad impetuous fool! That sounds amusing, but if you don't curb your caustic tongue on Wednesday you may end up surrounded by peevish and pouting colleagues and possibly a few wounds in your own emotional armour. Just because you're having to exercise a little patience that's no reason to take out your bad temper on others. Take extra special care when handling machinery today for you're too hasty for your own good.

THURSDAY, 8th. Your annual accounts will soon be expected, and even if your financial reckoning consists of counting the coppers in your pocket you should give some serious thought to ways and means of achieving a more secure economic base. Ruthlessly eliminate a system that hasn't worked too well in the past, as you'll easily replace it with a more efficient and effective one now. If in doubt consult an eminent expert who'll soon put you on the path to prosperity.

FRIDAY, 9th. You have every reason to feel quietly confident with the progress you've made in the employment market recently, especially when you realise how handy the extra cash is going to be. If you're having to fight for your rights against an unfair employer, this is a perfect time to consult a legal expert about your options, for they may have some very good news for you.

SATURDAY, 10th. How's your love-life these days? You may have been a bit busy with other matters to give the sexual and sensual side of life much attention recently, so seize today's chance to let your hair down and explore the erotic potential of a passionate partnership! Your composed public image conceals a lascivious streak that's as wild and wanton as the most lustful Lothario in the privacy of your own bedroom or imagination!

SUNDAY, 11th. Martial-minded Mars marches into your very own sign this Sunday and peps up the pace in your personal life until you'll hardly know if you're coming or going. It's time to take the brakes off in all projects that mean anything to you, from getting yourself into shape physically to presenting a much more assertive, aggressive and independent image. On a more private plane, there are emotional implications to a lustful liaison that must be brought out into the open.

MONDAY, 12th. It's all very well being the rebellious revolutionary of the zodiac, but there are times, like this Monday, when a subversive attitude is a positive disadvantage. The problem comes from the fact that so many folk are apt to misunderstand your dedication to the cause of freedom, and conclude that you're the enemy of law and order. That's not true, but it is up to you to convince confused companions of the fact. A tricky and taxing task!

TUESDAY, 13th. This is likely to be a much more profitable and productive day to do business and engage in high-level talks about the remuneration and rewards to be expected from a position you're thinking of taking on. It may be an official contract that's on the negotiating table or a less formal offer of professional advancement. Either way you should take all suggestions seriously and hold out for a just and fair settlement. Don't gloss over any of the financial details, for through being alert you could increase your profits.

WEDNESDAY, 14th. What a canny Water-carrier you can be at times! This is certainly one of your better days when it comes to organising a lush and lucrative deal for yourself with the powers that be, as inside information and the exploitation of behind the scenes contacts could land you a plum post. It may be professional promotion you seek or an opportunity to serve your community in a more official capacity, but either way your persistence will pay off handsomely now. You're a force to be reckoned with!

THURSDAY, 15th. As you gradually climb the steps of worldly success and status you've noticed that the way is seldom smooth and straightforward, and that is a useful piece of experience for it will stop you being thrown off your stroke by today's temporary turbulence. An unexpected emergency may bring on a crisis of conscience amongst unscrupulous Aquarians, but if you've nothing to be ashamed of you'll sail through this trifling storm with ease.

FRIDAY, 16th. With mental mastermind Mercury so ably supported by sensible Saturn today you should seize the opportunity to set your economic world in apple-pie order. Anything from arranging for a loan to help you invest in your future to working out a way of helping someone you admire and respect to get their head above water financially should be discussed, debated and registered whilst you're so shrewd. Money matters make marvellous progress now.

SATURDAY, 17th. Playtime! Even if you're an Aquarian who has to work over the weekends, you should ensure an outing or excursion this Saturday to keep your social circle spinning. It could be a wild and wonderful shindig in your own abode or an informal meeting of the gang at your local pub, club or hostelry. You may be busy but you must make time for your friends if you're to enjoy life to the full.

SUNDAY, 18th. Socially you're a real sensation this weekend as you continue to play the pleasant part of being the life and soul of every party that's going. If you're an Aquarian alone a friend you meet in the midst of Sunday's merrymaking may well turn out to be the love of your life, or at least a passionate playmate to while away a few amorous hours with. You're right at the top of the popularity stakes!

MONDAY, 19th. You may not be best friends with your bank manager, but you shouldn't shun his or her company if you're hoping to increase your economic activity in line with your ambitions. In fact any financial expert you talk to today should prove very amenable and agreeable as you're able to express your plans with such clarity and confidence. If the subtle science of money-management is a mystery to you, now is your chance to get informed and educated.

TUESDAY, 20th. Mercury makes a mad dash for your solar house of short journeys and communications, and simultaneously the Sun sets his seal of approval on your efforts to better yourself educationally. The result is a whole month when you'll be as busy as a summertime bee, bustling about making intriguing and informative new contacts and learning all there is to know about local and social affairs. When it comes to sheer cleverness you're beyond compare now!

WEDNESDAY, 21st. As you weave a subtle web of clandestine contacts amongst your colleagues and superiors you stand a very good chance of advancing your ambitions and taking a significant but secretive step closer to your ultimate goal. You intuitively understand the fundamental principles governing business and public affairs and this sets you in a class of your own careerwise, so why not deliver a discreet demonstration of your skills and expertise? You'll make quite an impression on the powers that be!

THURSDAY, 22nd. There are so many rumours flying around your workplace this Thursday that you'll need to take everything with a large pinch of salt until you see something in writing. It all sounds very promising, for it seems there's a new era of expansion and opportunity on the horizon, whether you're in an established occupation or still looking for your niche in life. Don't go overboard for the more optimistic options, but you can take a quietly confident approach.

FRIDAY, 23rd. You've had your fill of the bruising battle to make your way in the world and for once just want to sink into the welcoming arms of love and luxury, and why not! You've earned a break, so keep your schedule to an absolute minimum and make sure your evening is totally indulgent, enjoyable and undemanding. Snuggle up on the sofa with a passionate playmate and make an early start on the weekend's entertainments!

SATURDAY, 24th. It doesn't take you long to bounce back, does it?! You're full of beans and fighting fit this Saturday, fizzing over with enthusiasm for all your usual chores and any extra errands you have planned. An unexpected visitor may throw a spanner in the works for a wee while, so make sure your day's plan has plenty of leeway for sociable surprises!

SUNDAY, 25th. I wouldn't dream of interrupting your day of rest, but if you can spare a moment between lunch, your snooze on the sofa, and tea maybe you should give some thought to the direction your financial progress is taking? If you take a close look at the facts and figures involved in a novel notion a fiscally creative friend has put forward you may find there's more to it than meets the eye. Your economic intuition is at its best now.

MONDAY, 26th. It's high time you took an interest in your local affairs, as there are issues in the air now that affect your own environment and it's up to you to make sure you're fully informed about the implications. Anything from a welcome improvement in the civic amenities to a problem over planning permission for undesirable developments captures your attention and activates your social standards. You're such a conscientious member of your community!

TUESDAY, 27th. Someone will spin you a yarn today that sounds utterly convincing until you take a close look at the facts behind their fancy. You'll find there's no substance whatever in their accusations, enticements and innuendoes. They'll play on your sympathies and appeal to your uncompromising principles, but that's no reason to let them hoodwink you. Keep your head and don't sign anything now!

WEDNESDAY, 28th. You're not usually much of a home-bird, but under this Wednesday's sociable stars you're keen to make contact with your kith and kin, if only to make sure they're all getting along all right. You'll be glad you have made the effort, even if it means making a long-distance phone call or taking a drastic detour on your way home from work, as there's nothing to compare with the sensational sense of security to be derived from knowing that you belong.

THURSDAY, 29th. Now you're in touch with the further branches as well as the roots of your family tree you should make it your business to find out what the latest news is, for there are some fascinating developments amongst your relatives that will keep you enthralled. Anything from new babies born into the clan to kinsfolk who have taken up weird and wonderful activities will make you realise you're a member of a real go-ahead group! A long-lost relative may put in an appearance from out of the blue.

FRIDAY, 30th. The postmen will drop a bombshell through your letter-box today that'll have you in quite a tense tizzy all day as you digest the incredible implications of the news. Your immediate impulse is to try to bury your head in the sand rather than face up to the fact that something will never be the same again, but you'll find the whole experience much more exciting and exhilarating if you look on the bright side and work out ways to make the most of a change in your circumstances. Think before you speak on this disquieting day.

SATURDAY, 31st. You're prone to problems with your nerves, so seize the chance offered by this Saturday's sensational stars to totally forget your cares and concerns in order to let your hair down and relax. Whatever restores your sense of balance and well-being best, from a delicious candlelit dinner with a certain someone special to a day spent in the convivial company of a sporting crowd of chums should top your weekend agenda.

APRIL

SUNDAY, 1st. This is a superficially very pleasant day, filled with polite conversation and easy-going affection, but beneath the surface you're gripped by dark fears and unconscious apprehensions about your ability to hold your own in educated and cultured company. No one would guess that you were struggling to keep up your end of the exchange, for your acting skills are marvellous.

Your worries are weighing on you needlessly, for you're actually a very intelligent and accomplished Aquarian!

MONDAY, 2nd. Sudden symptoms that overtake you today may make you anxious and apprehensive about your health. There's no doubt that if you're ailing you should consult a medical expert without delay, but your imagination is inclined to be a little over-active and you could easily mistake a minor cold for a major catastrophe. Try to keep the amateur dramatics to a minimum and treat any health problems with a more sane and sensible attitude.

TUESDAY, 3rd. You've been treading a precarious path profes-sionally lately and as a result you have aroused the resentment of some very powerful people. They're quite capable of taking a crafty, cunning and crooked revenge so make sure your back is covered. So long as you don't sink to their deceitful and devious level and ensure your actions are all totally open and above board you'll be fine. Use extreme caution when dealing with anyone in authority now.

WEDNESDAY, 4th. You're entering an extended period of terrific domestic activity for mischievous Mercury enters your solar house of the hearth and home this Wednesday. It's a fantastic oppor-tunity to restore the bonds of affection between all the various branches of your clan as you'll find everyone's interested in know-ing everyone else's business and will warmly welcome any oppor-tunity to gossip and chat. Maybe you could organise a mammoth get-together for your kinsfolk? Any old excuse will do!

THURSDAY, 5th. Your one-to-one affairs will be clouded and confused due to the unwelcome presence of that green-eyed mon-ster, jealousy. On the face of it you know you have nothing to worry about, but there's a nagging suspicion that won't let you or your partner be until you've talked things through between you. Aquarians with a roving eye had better beware the eagle eye of a distrustful partner!

FRIDAY, 6th. The gentle and generous planet Venus glides gra-ciously into your solar house of wealth and worth on Friday, ushering in a time of plenty and prosperity in all economic affairs. The rich rewards of past efforts are yours at last, but if you want to put a little of your good fortune by for less opulent times you'll need a good deal of self-discipline or you'll blow the lot on tasty and tempting treats! If you are thinking of investing in the arts or antiques you should do well in the coming weeks.

SATURDAY, 7th. Take advantage of the weekend to ponder the words and behaviour of some professional associates and officials, for although all is superficially serene there's more to a given situation than meets the eye. By carefully unravelling the connections and connotations of clues you've noted in passing you could gain an important edge over any opposition. Put your superb sleuthing skills to work and you'll advance your ambitions.

SUNDAY, 8th. It's been a long winter and although we're theoretically leaving it behind you feel the need of the brighter skies and warmer winds of foreign parts. An early holiday could be just what the doctor ordered, but if exotic countries are only a pipe-dream in your economic climate perhaps you could take off for a mini-tour of the countryside within reach of your area and breathe in some fine fresh air?

MONDAY, 9th. Yesterday's excursion has left you fretful and fidgety, making it very difficult to concentrate on the tedious details of a mundane Monday. You need a change of scene if you're to operate at your best now, so if you can arrange to take off for the wide blue yonder you'll be in your element. Water-carriers who can't afford to fly from obligations and agreements will have to confine their wayward wanderings to the world of the imagination.

TUESDAY, 10th. An impulsive idea strikes you on Tuesday and all of a sudden you're convinced that the answer to your problems would be to uproot yourself and your family and seek out a more congenial community or make some radical and revolutionary changes to your current abode. It's all very sudden, but once the initial shock is over your kith and kin will see there is some sense in your words. You might even toy with the idea of emigrating.

WEDNESDAY, 11th. Waste no time in following up a professional lead that falls into your lap quite by chance as you'll take your rivals by surprise and could leap up several extra rungs of the ladder of success! Whatever you aim to achieve in the world, from academic eminence to success in your own terms, you could find that a roundabout route is your best bet now.

THURSDAY, 12th. You're motivated today by a powerful passion to make your mark on the world in a way that demands respect from one and all, whatever your particular profession or craft may be. You're prepared to pour your reserves of energy and determination into your ambitions unstintingly, putting paid to any opposition or competition with the sheer force of your will. In all worldly affairs you're a force to be reckoned with these days!

FRIDAY, 13th. You're not inclined to take the old superstitions seriously, for you're a child of our times with a much more modern outlook. You certainly won't find any evidence in the events of your fascinating and fulfilling day to justify any fears about the date as there's plenty of positive and promising potential in the heavens for you. An unexpected opening in your career should be followed up immediately, before you lose the advantage.

SATURDAY, 14th. A prosperous pal may be lots of fun, but are you sure you can afford their brand of entertainment and enjoyment? You hate to turn down an invitation on the grounds of poverty, but that's just what you must do if you're to keep on an even keel economically. A shopping spree in the company of a congenial comrade will turn up some mighty tempting items which could stretch your budget to the limit.

SUNDAY, 15th. Yesterday's expensive excursions have certainly eaten into your economic foundations, but a surprise discovery will ease the situation and put you back in the black. All the same, it's given you a bit of a shock to realise how close you came to financial failure, and that will weigh on you until you've worked out a more watertight system of money-management.

MONDAY, 16th. As if to make up for the indulgences of your

84

weekend you're ready to throw yourself body and soul into your everyday chores, whether you're in a high-powered job or tackling the housework that's accumulated lately. It's a gallant attempt to ease your conscience, but if you bite off more than you can chew you'll only end up by undermining your health. Steady as you go Aquarius!

TUESDAY, 17th. Words of wisdom uttered in an undertone by a supremely sagacious member of your family should be taken to heart as they really do know what they're talking about and can help you to unravel a puzzling problem in your private life. You may not want the world and his wife to know the intimate details of your concerns, so if necessary wait for a quiet and secluded moment to consult your family oracle.

WEDNESDAY, 18th. There's a bright green celestial light giving you the go-ahead this Wednesday so prepare to be swept off your feet in the happy and harmonious hustle and bustle of a very busy day. Any errands that you've been putting off should be attended to now for you're in no mood to take 'No' for an answer from anyone who tries delaying tactics. You'll be tired but happy by bedtime as you'll have accomplished so much and forged many new and very positive links with your neighbourhood.

THURSDAY, 19th. There's no escaping the fact that Thursday's stars denote a very important stage in your domestic and professional lives. There are stresses and strains that can no longer be suppressed as you struggle to balance your occupational ideals against the demands of your home life. Something's gotta give, so start to talk about your problems and let loose a torrent of words before you succumb to the mental pressures. Once you get a few things off your chest you'll see things in a much clearer light.

FRIDAY, 20th. The Sun sinks to the horoscopic area of hearth and home today and turns your attention to the more emotional areas of your life. In the month ahead you've a golden opportunity to reminisce about childhood memories, habits or obsessions that are no longer appropriate, for you have the creative power now to free yourself from the bonds of the past. A total reorganisation of your abode will reflect the new you and help reinforce your resolutions.

SATURDAY, 21st. This is a fine time to look at savings schemes, insurance policies and bank accounts in order to sort out your best economic options. Even if you feel you've got that area of your life cut and dried it won't hurt to keep abreast of modern developments. By juggling your cash and investments in a slightly more adventurous manner you stand to make a princely profit.

SUNDAY, 22nd. I know it's a day of rest, but it would be to your advantage to put in an appearance at a fairly formal gathering being organised amongst your professional peers. Even if you don't play an active part in the semi-sociable manoeuvring and manipulation that goes on you'll be able to observe the subtle way power is being wielded. Once you've worked out the pecking order you can benefit from your insights.

MONDAY, 23rd. Just because your kith and kin are used to your little ways you shouldn't take it for granted that they'll understand your every action without having it spelt out to them, especially now that madcap Mercury's taking a detour and generating confusion in all communications. Take time and trouble over explaining your ideas and your actions to your family and you'll save yourself plenty of needless muddle in the long run. Messages and letters are apt to go astray, so double-check everything important.

TUESDAY, 24th. There seems to be a psychological block sitting at the back of your mind, sowing surreptitious seeds of doubt and dismay. Subjects you thought you knew inside out suddenly become confused and clouded as your mind goes blank when faced with the simplest of tasks and topics. There's no need to assume that you're destined for a dull and dim-witted future, for this is a very fleeting phase and you'll very soon be back on your usual brilliant intellectual form!

WEDNESDAY, 25th. Home and family take the top priority in this Wednesday's astral agenda, as the Taurean New Moon accentuates your need to renew and renovate the roots of your world. Obstacles and assumptions laid down in your childhood have held you back for long enough, so seize on this chance to leave unwanted emotional hang-ups behind. If you're thinking of having radical rebuilding work done on your abode this is a fine time to begin.

THURSDAY, 26th. Any apprehension you had about the reaction of your nearest and dearest to changes you have planned to your home life will be delightfully dispelled today, for once they understand your reasoning your family will all rally round and applaud your initiative. Mention a few of your ideas to a colleague or companion and they'll come up with a list of useful contacts and recommended workmen who will come in very handy.

FRIDAY, 27th. A bureaucratic boss may make some heavy-handed demands on your time and energies today that will have you quietly simmering and smouldering at the tyrannical injustice of it all. Instead of taking it out on your long-suffering family you should take your grievances to the proper authorities and utilise the correct channel for complaints. You may think a lone voice like yours has no chance of being heard, but how do you know until you've tried?

SATURDAY, 28th. The congenial cause of fund and frolics has been pushed aside lately and now's your chance to resurrect it with a very warm welcome into your life. A luscious night out with a loved one or a visit to a ritzy restaurant will bring bliss bubbling benevolently to the surface. Don't make the mistake of thinking that pleasure can be measured in terms of the size of the bill, for you'll be much happier staying within the bounds of your budget.

SUNDAY, 29th. What are your long-term employment plans? Whatever your position on the scale of success and status you have the opportunity within your grasp of achieving some of your most avid and ardent ambitions if you take the trouble *now* to think out your targets and goals. You stand to increase your income through taking a more positive and persuasive line with potential employers, employees and clients, so don't play small when there's such a gloriously lucrative game afoot!

MONDAY, 30th. If you're planning to move house now is a brilliant time to view possible places and explore some domestic options you hadn't thought of before. Maybe you should consider setting up home in a houseboat or converting an old barn to suit your own particular tastes? There's no earthly reason to restrict yourself to an abode that looks like a million others in this country, so even if it's just going in for a little unusual and inventive décor you should make sure your home expresses your individuality.

MAY

TUESDAY, 1st. You've been forcing the pace a wee bit where changes in your home life are concerned, and today your sensitive emotional antennae will pick up on some of the concerns your family have. If you've any sense at all you won't dismiss their worries and fears out of hand, however irrational they may be, for through allowing your family to air their apprehensions you'll defuse a potentially difficult situation and help forge a stronger bond of trust and friendship between your kinsfolk. You're an intuitive ace now!

WEDNESDAY, 2nd. You're making great strides professionally these days as your sterling qualities of drive and determination finally receive the recognition they deserve, but there's a fly in the ointment in the form of a romantic or business partner who is eaten up with envy at the sight of your success. You're tempted to rub salt in the wound out of annoyance at their petty jealousy, but isn't that just as bad? Show a more magnanimous spirit and they'll forget their fears.

THURSDAY, 3rd. The more you ponder on the wonderful wealth this world has to offer to those who dare to take a few risks, the more eager you are to strike boldly out on a brand new and totally original venture. Follow a hunch, wherever it leads, even if it's not your usual employment scene, for through tuning in to your intuition you'll enhance your economic world and prosper most profitably. Your nearest and dearest have some very acute and useful observations to make so heed their advice.

FRIDAY, 4th. As Venus steps sweetly into your solar house of local and social affairs from this Friday you can expect a very pleasant period amongst acquaintances and associates who feel that you're definitely the flavour of the month! Take an avid interest in community affairs, especially if it involves improving the overall appearance of your neighbourhood for you'll easily win influential support to your side. Solo Water-Carriers should keep an eye open for the girl or boy next door, who could prove amorously very interesting!

SATURDAY, 5th. There's a heavy heavenly emphasis on your spiritual development these days, and this weekend brings the blossoming of a new awareness of your inner capacity for kindness and compassion. It may be the formal teaching of a religious leader who's captured your imagination or simply some standards you've worked out for yourself, but either way it is clear to you that you must give your psychic, supernatural and instinctive abilities an appropriate outlet. You're an inspired Aquarian!

SUNDAY, 6th. Call for a family forum or a gathering of the clan this Sunday, whether you've an occasion to celebrate or not, for you have some urgent business to discuss with everyone concerned and can't be expected to make some important decisions all on your own. It may be shared financial assets to be disposed of or a disputed inheritance to sort out, but you need not fear a clash or conflict for once the topic's been openly broached you'll find folk are very reasonable and fair-minded.

MONDAY, 7th. You covered a lot of ground yesterday in your talks with far-flung relatives, but are you sure there aren't certain strains and stresses in your immediate family you've been trying to brush under the carpet? It may be you or your nearest and dearest who are secretly seething with suppressed rage, so don't shirk the issue. You may have to face up to an ugly scene or two whilst you all get a few things off your chests, but it'll be worth it in the long run.

TUESDAY, 8th. No one likes to work in an environment that's dirty, dangerous or depressing, so if that's the state of your work-place you should organise a deputation of concerned colleagues and tackle the people in power with your positive proposals. You won't get far with a negative approach, but by presenting some potential options you'll win praise and admiration as well as achieving some much-needed improvements.

WEDNESDAY, 9th. The fulminating rays of today's Full Moon fill your world and force a radical review of your public image and ambitions. Are you achieving all you wish? Or are you more like the proverbial square peg in a round hole? You can no longer put up with a professional position or social status that does not reflect your true abilities and aptitudes, so set some wheels in motion to bring you into a more fulfilling era. Old aspirations must be modernised or discarded.

THURSDAY, 10th. There's no point in pretending to be rational and reasonable about monetary matter this Thursday as your emotions are inextricably involved in the sensitive subject of financial security. Altruistic and philanthropic sentiments direct your economic actions now, for you're deeply touched by the sad plight of the needy and want to support your sympathies with a decent donation. A surprise meeting with a rich relative could help swell your charitable gifts.

FRIDAY, 11th. Unemployed Aquarians should look on the bright side this Friday and follow up any lead offered through the family grapevine, however flimsy it appears at first sight. Lady Luck is on your side, especially if you're willing to investigate opportunities that seem too advanced for your abilities. You should never underestimate yourself, as you'll easily bluff your way through any problems or awkward questions and stand to land yourself the job of your dreams! If you're quite happy in your present position a new staff member may brighten up the atmosphere.

SATURDAY, 12th. Your worldly aims and ambitions have been under pulverising pressure from powerful Pluto for some time, and today you could reach a terrifically fortunate turning-point with the energetic aid of mighty Mars. You should prepare to push for a settlement of any outstanding obstacles to the achievement of your most cherished goals for you're in a fierce and forceful frame of mind and will easily defeat any opposition. What a determined dynamo you are!

SUNDAY, 13th. There's a clarion call across the heavens today, for there are personal and professional freedoms at sake. Your very own ruler, unpredictable Uranus, vies with gigantic Jupiter to produce the most opulent and unlimited openings and as a result the cause of modesty and moderation is completely lost. There are material, emotional and instinctive restrictions in your life that must be ditched forthwith, but try not to dictate the same terms to less adventurous folk, for they must make their own choices.

MONDAY, 14th. A cat on a hot tin roof has nothing on you this Monday as you restlessly roam around, bored with any activity that presents itself and unable to settle down to anything. You're distracted by an inner debate between contradictory feelings fighting for your full attention. It seems nonsensical, but the fact is that you're quite capable of entertaining several different emotions at once, so why try to pin yourself down? It's a losing battle anyway under today's turbulent sky.

TUESDAY, 15th. You'll fall prey to your most insidious anxieties and worrying fears this Tuesday if you don't make a positive effort to think positive. Mother Moon is frozen into a block of emotional ice by stern Saturn, making you feel totally cut off and isolated from all sources of warmth and affection. Your lonesome state is just a delusion however, and all it takes to shatter the illusion is to stretch out the hand of friendship to someone near.

WEDNESDAY, 16th. Theoretically you know there are some hard facts to be faced and pragmatic choices to be made, but it might be wiser to postpone all practicalities to a less wistful, winsome and weary day. You're much more suited to a day spent delving into the delights of your dream world, entertaining yourself with imaginative illusions and voluptuous visions. Don't deal with any documents relating to cash or possessions unless you have to, as there are dishonest folk around now.

THURSDAY, 17th. Someone in a position of authority over you

91

seems to take a perverse pleasure in making your life a misery as they play a subtle and sneaky game of manipulation and domination with your personal aims and ambitions. You're terribly tempted to set yourself up in opposition and exact a fitting revenge from them, but any such unworthy or ignoble activities will only rebound on your own reputation in the long run. Play a cool, calm and collected part and you'll prove yourself more than a match.

FRIDAY, 18th. I know you're not a materialist at heart, but you're not about to turn down an opportunity that comes your way today to earn a little extra cash and generally boost your income. If you dream of rolling in riches without lifting a finger actually to warrant such wealth you won't make much headway, but by being willing to put in the work required you'll reap some very opulent and affluent rewards. Opportunity knocks and canny Aquarians fling wide the door!

SATURDAY, 19th. If I were you I'd leave your wallet safe and secure at home, along with your cheque book and credit cards this Saturday, unless you can honestly afford to spend a fortune satisfying a sudden whim as you wander around the shops. There's a certain amount of danger from pickpockets and purse-snatchers too, so as a sensible precaution you should carry only the bare minimum of cash.

SUNDAY, 20th. If you did end up going a wee bit over your budget yesterday it might be worth asking a richer relative to help you out with an extra injection of cash, for your kinsfolk are inclined to be in a benevolent and bountiful mood. Show your appreciation by agreeing to do a few odd jobs around the house or in the garden and they may even consider you quits.

MONDAY, 21st. The springtime Sun enters the next stage in his progress around the zodiac today, introducing you to a merry and mirthful month of fun and frolics. Creatively you're about to reach a peak so whether you're considering a bonny new addition to the family or an artistic endeavour designed to make the most of your particular talents, now is the time to forge ahead with your pleasurable plans.

TUESDAY, 22nd. Whenever you're stumped, stymied or stopped in a personal project you should place the problem before your family as their combined experience and expertise will very quickly come up with a novel approach to help you overcome your obstacles. Talk to a relative about your own fascination with psychic, supernatural and spiritual phenomena and you could hear some enthralling and entrancing tales.

WEDNESDAY, 23rd. It seems that almost anything you say and do these days is calculated to rub up an over-sensitive official the wrong way and that's the situation once more this Wednesday. Part of the problem is down to your automatic opposition to anyone with an air of authority, for uneasy autocrats very quickly know when they've a born rebel on their hands. Try to curb your natural resistance to the bosses and bureaucrats of this world and you'll get along much better.

THURSDAY, 24th. There are secret fears and private anxieties holding you back these days, causing you to question your route and direction in life. You have a fine chance now to think things through or to talk them over with a close companion, so don't clam up when understanding and encouragement are at hand. Where spare-time pastimes are concerned you should initiate a creative venture destined to bring love, life and happiness into your world, from extra activity in the arts or news of a possible pregnancy.

FRIDAY, 25th. Feminine influences of all kinds should be given top priority on this fun-filled Friday as you'll find it is the women around you who are most understanding, easy-going and amusing. A love-affair that's had a rather shaky start will begin to blossom into a rapturous romance if you take the trouble to lavish some affectionate attention on the object of your desires. You amorous Aquarian!

SATURDAY, 26th. I hope you enjoyed yourself to the full yesterday for today's stars point to a parade of petty problems interrupting the free flow of affection. A mysterious message from someone you thought adored you seems very cool, but before you jump to the melancholy conclusion that they're giving you the push you should wait and give them a second chance. You're a soft touch for a sob story, but don't give more than you can easily manage.

SUNDAY, 27th. As you sit down with your family for a nice restful and relaxing day the conversation will come round to your job and your long-term prospects. You'd do well to listen closely to any advice that's offered in a friendly and informal way for you'll pick up some terrific tips and very handy hints. An old friend of the family who has made good will take an encouraging interest that may lead to a highly profitable and prestigious position. This is no day to clam up and keep your own counsel!

MONDAY, 28th. A lead you were given over yesterday's lunch or high tea should be entered at the top of your schedule today as it always pays to strike while the iron is hot. However humble your family background may be, there are some situations when you'll gain plenty of cachet and clout from dropping a few names, so get weaving and promote yourself in a positive light.

TUESDAY, 29th. Your close personal partnerships must be treated with extra tact, diplomacy and discretion this Tuesday, whether it's a platonic pal or a passionate playmate you're dealing with. Just about everyone you care about is apt to be super-sensitive and easily upset and it's up to you to steer a careful course around any upsetting issues or sore spots. You'll earn oodles of affectionate gratitude if you take their fretful feelings into account.

WEDNESDAY, 30th. Domestically speaking you're in for a span of absolute joy and happy harmony as the luscious lady of the skies, velvet Venus, glides gracefully into your solar house of hearth and home. Peace and concord reign supreme in your abode during the coming weeks, giving you an excellent opportunity to heal any rifts between your relatives and to unite your family in a common cause of universal affection. A fantastic patch for kissing and making up!

THURSDAY, 31st. Your life is about to take on a fast and furious pace as ever-active Mars hastens hotfoot into your house of communications. Until mid July you should launch yourself whole-heartedly into an all-out social campaign, whether you're keen to contact the live wires of your locale or find out more concerning the network of news in your neighbourhood. If you stop talking long enough to listen to others as well as holding forth about your own views you'll win some firm friends and influence important people.

JUNE

FRIDAY, 1st. You're not a secretive soul by nature, but even the most frank and forthright Water-Carrier must have a few private and personal mysteries. Under today's reticent, reflective and reserved astral array you'll be inclined to keep your plans very close to your chest, and that's all to the good. If you've been feeling under the weather recently you should heed the advice of a friend or loved one and seek some professional help to sort yourself out.

SATURDAY, 2nd. I think the faint scent of summer in the air has gone straight to your head, for you're full of the joys of life and fizzing over with boundless energy. Anyone who makes the mistake of trying to calm you down runs the risk of feeling the sharp edge of your tongue as you've no time at all for people lacking in imagination or a sense of adventure. You'll be in your element dashing hither and thither on all kinds of interesting errands, but don't be in too much of a hurry to observe the safety codes on the roads.

SUNDAY, 3rd. You're not one of the most timid and timorous souls in the zodiac dozen gang, but you're no fool either and know when to keep your distance as a rule. Still, rules are made to be broken, especially by rebellious Aquarians, so today you're apt to bite off far more than you can chew whilst rushing into a sensitive situation that really requires far more tender and tactful treatment. Steer well clear of touchy and temperamental folk.

MONDAY, 4th. All you really want to do now the summer's on the horizon is to roam free and explore the many wonders this world has to offer, but are you sure you've not forgotten something important that might spoil all your fun? An early vacation could be ruined by a nagging doubt about overlooked obligations and neglected duties so double-check all arrangements and bookings until you've set your mind at rest.

TUESDAY, 5th. You were never cut out for a plodding and prosaic profession for you're far too spirited and individualistic to stick to a strict nine to five routine. If you've drifted into working practices that are beginning to hem you in and instil some hateful habits you should set your mind to the problem now. If you use your intuition and think along original lines you should find a way to have your cake and eat it be keeping your current position whilst reorganising the schedule to suit your own taste for variety. Canny!

WEDNESDAY, 6th. You've done some pretty inspiring work on your abode recently and now the hard graft is complete you have a chance to turn your artistically excellent attentions to the décor now. What you have in mind is an up to the minute effect, far from the boring beauties of traditional tastes, and with your superb ability to pick out the best in modern design you should end up with an abode that is way ahead of its time! On the work and health front you shouldn't believe all you hear for you're apt to be blinded by your idealism and wishful thinking.

THURSDAY, 7th. Thursday morning dawns full of vim, vigour and vitality, ready to launch you headlong into life. You're all fired up with avid enthusiasm for a worthy cause you've recently espoused, so rustle up some go-ahead pals who can help you achieve your altruistic aims. Social contacts of all kinds may provide the basis for personal and professional success now. Mentally you're as sharp as a razor and able to cut through the confusion to formulate a positive plan for the future.

FRIDAY, 8th. A forthright friend who cares enough to be really blunt with you may touch a raw nerve, but you'll thank them in the end for they have opened your eyes to the true feelings that lie behind some of most cherished objectives. Get down to brass tacks and decide once and for all what you want to achieve, for there are some activities that are just a waste of your precious time. Your kith and kin will have some superbly sensible comments to add that'll help you see things in their proper perspective.

SATURDAY, 9th. Mother Moon meanders moodily into your horoscope's house of dreams and fantasy this Saturday, filling your mind with the music of the spheres and luring you into the intensely private and mysteriously magical world of your own imagination. You're kindness personified when it comes to looking after someone in the grip of an emotional upset, but don't neglect your own inner needs. Calm contemplation is all you crave now.

SUNDAY, 10th. Maybe you should consider taking up a relaxation technique such as yoga or meditation? I mention it because you're apt to suffer from your nerves and today you'll be wound up as tight as a watch-spring if you don't allow yourself any let-up. Anything from a migraine to a spot of high blood pressure could result from pushing yourself physically and emotionally, so take pity on your troubled body and tense mind and learn to relax!

MONDAY, 11th. Anyone who dares to disagree with a pet belief of yours is in for a rough time on Monday as you jump down their throats and give them a tongue-lashing they'll never forget. It may have been unwise of them to tackle you on a topic so dear to you, but don't you think you're over-reacting just a teensy bit? Of course you are, so why don't you apologise and offer to discuss the matter coolly and calmly? They'll be a little wary but once you win back their confidence you could have a fascinating and informative chat.

TUESDAY, 12th. Anyone who doubted the creative power of your mind needs only to watch from the sidelines in the coming weeks, for your skills of self-expression are second to none. Whether it's amateur dramatics, a spot of spare-time painting or an interest in fine literature that inspires you, now is your chance to make your mark and advance your projects. There's a battle royal brewing on your domestic scene over some trivial incident that has sparked off old rivalries, and if I were you I'd stand well clear until the dust has settled.

WEDNESDAY, 13th. It is time you took a long hard look at your professional prospects and employment experiences in order to ascertain what your next move should be. Even if you're blissfully happy as you are nothing stays the same for ever and by anticipating events you stand to gain extra prestige and prosperity. This is the perfect opportunity to make a determined bid for the big time.

THURSDAY, 14th. At first sight you'd think all the ways of making money in this world had already been thoroughly explored and exploited, but that's reckoning without your original and inventive mind, my friend! It might mean something as simple as putting your savings into an unusual account with extra interest rates, or if you're an economic expert, you could work out a complex scheme to put you in the millionaire bracket. All it takes is a little lateral thinking, intuition and the courage of your convictions!

FRIDAY, 15th. Whether you're wealthy or as poor as a church mouse you should seriously consider coming up with the cash to finance an ambitious venture at your workplace. Maybe you have a chance to buy shares in your company, or simply want to invest in some equipment that'll make your life a lot easier. Either way it will be money well spent as you'll realise when the rewards start to flood in.

SATURDAY, 16th. The trouble with spending money is that it can get to be a habit and that's your problem on Saturday as you dig ever deeper into your personal piggy bank to finance a fun-filled weekend. By all means enjoy yourself, for you've earned a few luxuries and treats, but don't go overboard and lavish costly gifts on all and sundry for you'll regret your prodigality when the reckoning comes. Go easy on the expenses!

SUNDAY, 17th. Normally Sunday is a very welcome day of rest, but that's far too obvious and unexciting for you as all you want to do is take off for the wide blue yonder and experience as many brand new sights and sounds as possible. A surprise visit to some long-neglected pals seems like a brilliant idea at the time, but make sure you're not intruding too much on their much needed rest and relaxation. Maybe a trip to the seaside or into town would be more enjoyable? You just can't sit still now!

MONDAY, 18th. You're on the ball mentally this Monday, ready to tackle everything from the everyday errands and mundane chores to thinking out a long-term strategy for the attainment of your ambitions. Everyone you speak to will prove kind and cooperative as they're just as interested as you in keeping things flowing along smoothly. Don't expect earth-shaking events, but rather a steady rate of progress.

TUESDAY, 19th. By contrast today's stars are very tricky and treacherous indeed and if I were you I'd be extremely careful about the words you utter and the people you talk to. You're quite likely to let slip an item of classified information that'll cause no end of trouble if it gets out. Strangers who come to your door should be regarded with a certain amount of suspicion and scepticism. If in doubt as for the support of your family for they'll quickly see through any dishonest plot.

WEDNESDAY, 20th. As the fog clears from your brain you can clearly see there is some urgent action to be taken to clear up any misunderstandings and muddles that have arisen. Candidly own up to any mistakes you've made yourself and cheerfully point out the errors in someone else's understanding of a certain situation. They'll thank you for taking the initiative.

THURSDAY, 21st. Being such a highly charged and unpredictably energetic sign you often burn yourself out or place a sudden strain on your health and vitality, and from this Thursday you have an opportunity to assess the physical damage and do something about getting yourself back in the pink once more. Give yourself a medical MOT or consult an expert about any ailments you're puzzled about. A new employment era may also dawn now if that's something you seek.

FRIDAY, 22nd. The celestial spotlight is fiercely focused on your working world this Friday as the New Moon astrally urges you to sweep away negative influences and situations in your working world in order to make a more positive new beginning. If you're looking for a job this could be your lucky day, whereas working Water-carriers have a chance to make some much needed improvements and changes in their working agreements.

SATURDAY,23rd. Your subconscious mind has quite a few turbulent tricks up its sleeve in the form of forgotten fears and irrational impulses. There are certain emotional hang-ups that lie at the root of your most rebellious feelings and until you can work out just what they are and give them a more open expression they'll continue to upset your equilibrium. Look within for a clue to a disturbing or distressing situation.

SUNDAY, 24th. Sometimes it seems that your revolutionary role is just a cover-up for more deeply rooted fears that you're reluctant to face up to, and that's apparent this Sunday. Your blustering and bullying mood has vanished into thin air, leaving you sad and subdued and at the mercy of some inner anxieties that undermine your confidence. Treat yourself gently and don't take your indigo mood too seriously for it will soon lift, leaving you full of beans once more.

MONDAY, 25th. Velvet Venus floats flirtatiously into your horoscope's house of red-hot romance and playful passions from Monday, inaugurating a time of amorous entertainment and affectionate enjoyment. Solo Aquarians may very soon be pierced by one of Cupid's ardent arrows, but if love leaves you cold you should concentrate on an artistic interest. Children will show what little angels they can be for a while.

TUESDAY, 26th. Honest and open communications are crucial to all close relationships, from your marriage to a business association, so don't put up with personality clashes or unresolved resentments when by talking things over in a frank and forthright way you can so easily and effortlessly restore the peace. An urgent message may need to be given top priority.

WEDNESDAY, 27th. As the heavens' wizard with words, mini Mercury, enters your area of work and health you're granted the silver-tongued charm required to impress potential employers and colleagues with your intelligence and acumen. This is a splendid period for organising appointments and interviews in order to advance your aims and ambitions. Talking to medical experts and fitness consultants will also give you some valuable ideas.

THURSDAY, 28th. An intimate affair may be steering very close to the rocks as you and your passionate partner try to pretend that all's well when it isn't. You hate to open up an emotional can of worms as it's not in your nature to inquire too closely into fraught feelings, but for once you should make the effort to dig a little deeper than usual into your inner anxieties. You'll find the problem is not nearly as complicated as you'd supposed.

FRIDAY, 29th. You try to promote a public image that is completely cool, calm and collected, but you and I know that beneath the surface you're in an uproar as contradictory and conflicting impulses threaten to tear you in two. You can see that in order to make your way in the workaday world you'll need to maintain certain sane and sensible standards of behaviour, but in your heart of hearts you want to kick over the traces and indulge your wildest and wackiest whims. Some kind of compromise will have to be struck.

SATURDAY, 30th. What a supremely sensitive Saturday this is! The harsh world of everyday reality holds no appeal for you now as you dwell in the delightful domain of delicious day-dreams. A sophisticated and civilised day out taking in the cultural classics, whether that means a night at the opera or strolling round a magnificent museum will be right up your street, for you need to surround yourself with the very best this world has to offer. What a refined soul you are!

JULY

SUNDAY, 1st. It seems obvious to you that the most surprising, shocking and startling ideas are usually the best and if anyone tries to persuade you that a more moderate view has its merits this Sunday you'll be up in arms about their mediocre modesty. As far as you're concerned it's better to go down with all guns blazing rather than feebly fade away. You have a point, but don't act the innocent if others disagree!

MONDAY, 2nd. On the work-front you're a model of efficiency and effectiveness this Monday, fully informed and up to date on every situation affecting your job. On a deeper level you're not nearly so bright and breezy however, as you're struggling with secret fears and unconscious apprehensions about your own competence. You're being blocked from making the best uses of your excellent abilities and the solution to your worries lies within!

TUESDAY, 3rd. You're at the mercy of an inner emotional confusion this Tuesday, for you're mentally and emotionally undermined by a dismaying deluge of doubt about your own aptitudes and skills. You're determined to get to the bottom of your mysterious moods, but you could end up going round and round in confusing circles if you demand too much of yourself mentally. The dividing line between fact and fiction is blurred and broken now.

WEDNESDAY, 4th. Don't suffer in silence, whether it's an unsatisfactory working arrangement or physical ailments which are plaguing you this Wednesday, for by taking your grievance to the top you'll meet with an understanding and helpful response. Negotiations with the powers that be to give you a greater degree of personal responsibility and freedom should be pursued in a persistent and professional way. Impress them with your grasp of the implications and you'll gain their confidence and trust.

THURSDAY, 5th. The golden glow of the summer sun is dimmed and diffused by a Neptunian cloud of chaotic confusion today, and the resulting gloom covers your entire working world with a worrying aura of anxiety and uncertainty. You're tempted to strike out against people or circumstances that seem to be bringing you down, but quite honestly you can't be bothered, and even if you did you'd find yourself on very shaky ground. Lie low and wait for clearer skies.

FRIDAY, 6th. Friday morning dawns full of eagerness and enthusiasm, ready to launch you head first into any challenge that comes along. A fun-loving friend will help you formulate a plan to achieve some of your most heartfelt hopes so don't keep your aims and objectives strictly to yourself. By bragging and boasting to all and sundry you'll gather a positive and optimistic band around to keep you on course. Socially you're the bees' knees!

SATURDAY, 7th. Loquacious Mercury is given a new zest for living this Saturday by jocular Jupiter as they hold a heavenly get-together in your solar house of work and well-being. A chance remark by someone you meet informally will put you on the trail of the job of your dreams, so however far-fetched it may seem, you should follow up each and every lead. Good news about a health problem is on the way too.

SUNDAY, 8th. You're psychically superb this Sunday, intuitively aware of any emotional undercurrents that subconsciously shape your reactions and responses. This is your chance to rid yourself of a complex or compulsion that's controlled you for far too long, so dig deeply into your inner emotional workings. Pay no heed to a comrade who tries to tell you it's impossible, for what do they know?

MONDAY, 9th. You're as keen as mustard to get your instinctive insights and intuitive understanding into words that anyone can understand, but it's not as easy as you thought. It seems simple and obvious enough to you, but either you've picked some very obtuse people to confide in or you're just not expressing yourself clearly. Part of the problem is your own impatience, for you must accept that complicated concepts take time to get across.

TUESDAY, 10th. Few things get your goat quite as much as incompetent officials or people prone to abuse a position of power, so with the prospects indicated by this Tuesday's confrontational sky you can expect to be in a cross and cantankerous mood for much of the day. You have a point about the parlous state of the world, but aren't you taking it all a wee bit too seriously? A little light-hearted laughter will help you put any problems back in perspective.

WEDNESDAY, 11th. You're suddenly struck today by how much your spouse or any other close companions have to say for themselves, for you're entering a period when your partnerships of all kinds are perked up by the articulate influence of the galaxy's chatterbox, wee Mercury. It's a fantastic opportunity to catch up on what your other half truly thinks, for the lines of communication are wide open. Before you launch yourself into a heart to heart there are some urgent errands to be attended to without delay.

THURSDAY, 12th. A fierce and ferocious-looking Mars steps up the pressure domestically and could stir up a hornets' nest of prodigious proportions in the process. There are diverse and divergent desires dominating the various factions of your family, and the only way to prevent an outbreak of furious feuding is to get things out in the open as quickly as possible. Channel your excess energies into some strenuous home improvements or a bit of building work.

FRIDAY, 13th. You can safely ignore the ominous overtones of today's date, but there are emotional undercurrents disturbing the smooth waters of your world that can't be so easily overlooked. An unresolved problem rooted in past emotional experiences may result in physical symptoms if you don't make a determined effort to gain a more realistic and balanced sense of proportion. A tense and tiresome time, when you should address yourself to important personal issues.

SATURDAY, 14th. Rationally, you know perfectly well that you have very little to worry about, for even if you have personal problems you're easily up to the challenge of dealing with them effectively. That's not much help when you're deluged by doubts and overwhelmed by anxious apprehensions that have been with you for a very long time. It's a useful opportunity for you to assess the strength of certain hang-ups you're harbouring, but don't expect to forge ahead in any less personal projects.

SUNDAY, 15th. It's a good thing you're an adaptable Aquarian, as Sunday's stars shine with the lovely light of pure enthusiasm and inspiring optimism! Gaze gleefully into the far future and consider your ultimate employment aims . . . maybe you should take the board of directors as your target, or aim for eminence as the best in your particular field? This is not time to mess about with piddling or puny ambitions when there's a whole world of opportunity laid out at your feet!

MONDAY, 16th. If you're not out at work it might be wise to arrange for a day out just to keep you out of the hair of your kith and kin. They may be precious to you, but your nearest relatives have some very irritating little ways, and for that matter some of your mannerisms seem to drive others wild on this moody Monday. Don't give in to a spiteful temptation to lash out just to relieve your furious feelings, it'll only make matters worse.

TUESDAY, 17th. You have your eager eyes on a highly desirable professional prize this Tuesday, but there are jealous people in your family who will try to sabotage your success if you're not on red alert. It all seems most unfair that they should choose this crucial time to burden you with their unhappy emotions, but you'll get nowhere by burying your head in the sand and hoping they'll let you be. Ruthlessly root out any opposition to your ambitions.

WEDNESDAY, 18th. Aquarians on vacation should be in for a delightful day now, as the heavens herald a time of terrific two-somes and fun-filled frolics. If sun, sand and sea are just a far-fetched dream to you maybe you should break the hold of the mid-week blues by treating your other half to a night out on the tiles? Even if you only have the time and energy for a wander down to your local pub or club you'll feel refreshed and restored by the change of scene.

THURSDAY, 19th. There are tender times when even the most wayward and wilful Water-Carrier wants to revel in the raptures of romance, and that's true for you today. If there's no one handy to help make your heart beat with a pounding pulse of passion maybe you should spend time with babies, children or youngsters, as their refreshingly innocent outlook on life will fill you with hope for the future.

FRIDAY, 20th. The luscious and loving Lady of the skies, velvet-een Venus, steps seductively into the centre stage of your working world this Wednesday, ushering in a pleasant period when happy and harmonious relations with colleagues and bosses takes top priority. You'll cross swords with a peevish partner if you insist on getting your own way and totally ignore their wishes, so let the spirit of compromise play an important part in all relationships.

SATURDAY, 21st. Everyone you meet and talk to about your occupational options these days has nothing but encouragement and optimism to offer, but for some reason that doesn't make you feel any better. In your innermost thoughts you're secretly afraid that you won't be able to live up to the positive potential everyone else sees as yours for the taking. Don't let false modesty and unfounded fears prevent you from using your advantages to the full.

SUNDAY, 22nd. You're not about to brag about it from the rooftops, but you're actually operating at genius level this Sunday. Use your astonishingly accurate intuition to sort out an intricate economic mystery and you'll earn the gratitude and respect of the experts. Recent developments on the health front have made it crystal clear to you that it's time you took a fresh look at the way you look after yourself physically. Update your regime and you'll soon be fighting fit!

MONDAY, 23rd. The radiance of the summer Sun spills over into your relationships-house from the early hours of this morning, illuminating your one-to-one affairs with brilliant beams and bountiful blessings. If you're already wed this is a fine time to reaffirm your vows and ensure that you and your other half are still a terrific team. If you're alone and lonesome you've a magical month to find yourself a suitable soul mate!

TUESDAY, 24th. A sizzling sky crammed with sensual, sexy and sensitive stars activates your most delicious desires and instigates an erotically enchanting interlude. Ooh la la! If you're just not turned on by the prospect of physical passion you should channel your passionately persistent energies into uncovering the true facts about a legal loophole associated with your economic interests. By aggressively asserting your rights you stand to make a pretty penny.

WEDNESDAY, 25th. Unruly Cupid had cast a whole quiverful of ardent amorous arrows your way this Wednesday, and the romantic result is liable to be chaotic and confusing in the extreme as you find yourself irresistibly attracted to people who just don't fit your usual stylish standards. Before you declare undying adoration

106

and fling yourself at the feet of a startled stranger you should wait a wee while to see if a passion born under such an unpredictable sky really has a hold on your heart. You mad, romantic fool you!

THURSDAY, 26th. I should think you'll be really quite relieved to hear that Thursday's sky offers nothing more challenging or exciting than a few quiet words about a clandestine matter and a pleasant exchange with a chatty colleague. It's an excellent opportunity to catch up on paperwork or errands that have been neglected lately, as well as restoring your inner sense of emotional equilibrium.

FRIDAY, 27th. Holiday time is upon us and all of a sudden you'll find yourself faced with the task of getting yourself organised for your annual outing. Your good intentions about being properly prepared in good time seem to have gone by the board, but it won't help matters to rush around in a frantic frenzy. An unexpected opportunity to take an extra vacation must be looked at carefully for there may be a catch.

SATURDAY, 28th. If you're travelling to your dream holiday this Saturday you must be careful not to build up your hopes too high, for nowhere on earth can totally reach your every ideal. By being reasonably realistic about your expectations, you're more likely to be pleasantly surprised than disappointed by the scene that confronts you on your arrival. Don't demand too much of yourself healthwise just now.

SUNDAY, 29th. As mastermind Mercury makes his way into your house of subversive secrets so you suddenly put a sock in it and keep your thoughts as close to your chest as possible. To an uninformed watcher you appear to be oblivious to your surroundings, but in fact you're an extraordinarily acute and accurate observer now. It's just that you don't see why you should squander the valuable resource of certain items of information on ignorant ears.

MONDAY, 30th. You're always keen to do your bit to help someone who has drifted into difficulties, but there are some people around on this Monday who may really need professional advice and support. Anything from a friend who's deeply dependent on drugs to a pal who's on the point of despair over a broken romance activates your most compassionate ideals. Don't delude yourself into thinking you can deal with something when in fact you're a long way out of your depth.

TUESDAY, 31st. Now you've assessed the situation that caused you so much confusion yesterday, the correct course of action is obvious to you and you'll set about doing right by anyone in need of aid at once. Don't hesitate to ask for extra advice from your family about how best to help someone who's struggling, for they'll back your charitable impulses to the hilt. You're up in arms about an injustice and for once you can do something positive to put matters right. You're living proof that gallantry is not dead!

AUGUST

WEDNESDAY, 1st. Just because you're often in competition with your colleagues for the plum jobs or most enjoyable tasks does not mean that they'll sell you down the river when an opportunity arises, for that is far from the truth. In fact Wednesday's experiences will reveal to you the strength available through solidarity with your workmates, so put personal differences to one side in the interest of making powerful progress as a team.

THURSDAY, 2nd. This is no time to be a dispassionate or disinterested Water-Carrier, for it is in the congenial company of your friends that you'll feel most at home on this sensitive Thursday. If your personal pals are few and far between, maybe you should consider joining an organisation or society devoted to a cause that strikes you as important? You'll soon meet up with some like-minded folk who'll welcome you as a friend and associate.

FRIDAY, 3rd. You're quite accustomed to being the bearer of bright ideas, but a brainwave that strikes you today will surprise even you by its sheer brilliance. You couldn't explain the source of your stupendous intellect, for intuition plays a prominent part in your mental processes, but no one can deny that you're the tops when it comes to thinking up ingenious and innovative solutions to a tricky problem.

SATURDAY, 4th. Don't be too cocksure about your ability to take on the big guns in a professional confrontation that's brewing, for you'll be treading a very dangerous path if you think you can challenge the combined might of all officialdom with impunity. A little humility wouldn't go amiss when dealing with the powers that be. You need to stand up for certain rights, but don't issue an open challenge.

SUNDAY, 5th. You really are irrepressible aren't you? I warned you about being too ebullient and bombastic, but you just carry on regardless as if the world really is your oyster. Over-confidence could be your downfall one of these days if you don't learn to restrict your actions to the bounds of reality. Your chief problem this Sunday is happily confined to the uncomfortable physical effects of over-indulgence.

MONDAY, 6th. Full Moon power permeates your sign, signalling the fact that you've come full circle in a personal project and must leave yourself out of the rut. It may be your appearance that needs a face-lift or your outlook on life that requires restoration and renewal – whatever the source of dissatisfaction, you must close the door on the old you and welcome a more fulfilling identity. Romantically you're in the doldrums, and need to break through a solid barrier of doubt and anxiety that's keeping you from the experience of affection.

TUESDAY, 7th. You're in good company this Tuesday, for the other fixed signs of the zodiac (Taurus, Leo and Scorpio) are also experiencing a time of tremendous tensions and monumental changes. Look to your ego and accept the fact that you'll get nowhere without taking the desires of your other half into account. It is very irksome and irritating to know you can't have an entirely free hand in achieving all you want, but the sooner you come to terms with the fact that you're not a free agent the better.

WEDNESDAY, 8th. Psychic, supernatural and occult interests dominate your mind today. You're utterly entranced by any subject or story that exudes an aura of magic and mystery, but far from being a naïve sucker your inquiring mind will be able to unravel many of the perplexing puzzles that you probe. You're intuitively inspired now, whether you believe in the potent power of the unconscious mind or not!

THURSDAY, 9th. What's the precise state of your personal finances? If that's a question that sets you scratching your head in baffled bewilderment it's high time you took a long hard look at your money-management system, for it's obviously failing to keep you adequately informed. Even if you know the size of your incomings and outgoings to the last detailed decimal, it wouldn't hurt to check over your figures and see if you can squeeze a little extra income from your assets and investments.

FRIDAY, 10th. A discreet discussion with someone who's wielding a good deal of power over you personally as well as in the world at large will work wonders in making sure that your interests are taken into account. If you make it clear without making a song and dance about it that you fully appreciate the difficulties of their position, but nevertheless feel you're entitled to a little extra consideration, you will prove your mastery of the ways of the world.

SATURDAY, 11th. What a cheerful, chatty and chirpy day! Why not don your prettiest frock or most elegant evening wear and take yourself off to some sizzling night-spot! You're sure to be the life and soul of any party that's going now, so if your diary is devoid of entertaining opportunities you'll just have to issue a few invitations yourself and organise an informal gathering at your place. You're in your element surrounded by a convivial crowd of revellers now.

SUNDAY, 12th. A charming colleague who has entered your life has completely captivated you with their winning ways, and if you're a solitary soul this could be the beginning of something big! If romance is out of the question you'll still want to bask in the bonds of affection that have been woven between you and your workmates. Watch out for signs of envious aggression from your other half though!

MONDAY, 13th. Put in plenty of hard graft on today to support your most deeply desired ambitions and you'll have good cause to feel quietly confident about your chances of making it through to the big time. Today also marks the beginning of a blissfully happy and harmonious span in your one-to-one affairs so don't let any amorous or affectionate opportunities pass you by. Anything from a second honeymoon to a brand new romance will fit the bill beautifully.

TUESDAY, 14th. If you've been following a personal policy of all work and no play you should make some far-reaching changes to your outlook on life, for if you take your nose away from the grindstone you'll catch sight of a delightful vista of enjoyable openings spread out at your feet. If you're married your other half will be instrumental in pointing out the importance of the pursuit of pleasure in a well-balanced and sensible lifestyle. Let your hair down and live a little!

WEDNESDAY, 15th. You had such a good time yesterday that you're more than ready to continue your entertaining education today. If you can get out and about once more so much the better, but if not you should begin to develop a personal pastime or spare-time hobby to keep you amused in your leisure hours. Maybe some craftwork or an artistic interest you've abandoned since schooldays is due for a revival? You're creatively commendable now.

THURSDAY, 16th. Common sense is a precious commodity that is often in very short supply once we eccentric Aquarians get a bee in our bonnet, but that's not true of even the wildest Water-Carrier on Thursday. Through thinking things out and laying careful plans down to the last detail concerning your worldly aims and aspirations you'll create for yourself a firm foundation of certainty and security to support you in your ambitious efforts.

FRIDAY, 17th. Get together with some serious-minded colleagues or concerned comrades and tackle someone in a position of authority about promised improvements in your everyday environment that just haven't happened. You'll naturally meet with an evasive and vague answer at first but if you persevere and demonstrate your determination to take your complaints to the very top you'll win a notable victory in the fight for justice.

SATURDAY, 18th. One of the heavens most magnificent inhabitants, genial Jupiter, moves his massive bulk into your solar house of close personal partnerships on Saturday, auguring an entire annum filled to overflowing with extra opportunities to enjoy the raptures of romance and the pleasures of tender togetherness. Current relationships are about to bloom and blossom, while solo Aquarians will find they're spoilt for amorous choice!

SUNDAY, 19th. There's a residue of resentment left in a business partnership that is all down to jealousy and envy on the part of someone who should know better. It will poison the potential for future collaboration and cooperation if you don't take steps to ease the tensions right now. Don't delay out of a foolish sense of pride, for you're selling yourself short if you simply accept such an unsatisfactory state of affairs.

MONDAY, 20th. If you're contemplating tying the knot with someone you've fallen for hook, line and sinker then you couldn't pick a more pertinent and proper time. There's a nuptial New Moon bringing a blissful new beginning into all one-to-one affairs, helping you to see just where you want your partnerships to go and how to achieve your amorous aims. Is that the sweet sound of wedding bells I hear?

TUESDAY, 21st. A snippet of inside information that comes your way this Tuesday may have profound implications for your career, however innocuous and innocent it appears at first glance. Follow up any such clues with single-minded determination as you could uncover a plot amongst unscrupulous competitors. Your immediate superiors will be as pleased as punch with your dogged detective work, and that'll stand you in very good stead when the prospect of promotion arises.

WEDNESDAY, 22nd. A special someone who whispers sweet nothings in your shell-like ear will seduce you from the straight and narrow at the drop of a hat, for where such sweet and seductive temptations are concerned your resistance is zero! Don't

112

hesitate to use your privileged position in the passions of someone who's a big noise in your profession to find out a few trade secrets. You can use any inside information to enhance your economic position.

THURSDAY, 23rd. It will quickly become obvious today that you're entering an emotionally intense and uncompromising era, making it increasingly difficult for you to ignore any inner impulses and fervent feelings. Take the lid off your emotions over a complex sexual situation, for you've an excellent opportunity now to unburden yourself of any intimate anxieties. A joint fiscal affair is about to move into a more prosperous phase.

FRIDAY, 24th. If you're off on your holidays this Friday I'd advise you to take a good book and plenty of snacks along for the journey, as there's a good deal of delay and diversion suggested by the heavens. It doesn't sound very auspicious, I know, but there's no earthly reason why a slow start to your vacation or your weekend should put you off. Don't let a mood of doom and gloom take hold, for it's not based on anything substantial.

SATURDAY, 25th. Be precise, particular and painstaking if you're dealing with important documents or agreements relating to a large-scale financial transaction. It is so easy to overlook a vital detail, especially now that young master Mercury has decided to go walkabout, resulting in a plethora of misunderstandings and mistakes. For the coming month you'll need to make extra sure you've dotted your 'i's and crossed your 't's.

SUNDAY, 26th. Stubborn, obstinate and intransigent are all ways of describing your attitudes this Sunday, as you're convinced there are people in your world who are out to tie you down and restrict your freedom. Your intractable approach will wreck a beautiful relationship if you don't get down from your high horse and admit that the situation is not as cut and dried as you are insisting. Give and take is crucial to all one to one contacts, and that doesn't mean you can do all the taking!

MONDAY, 27th. All's far from quiet on the home front today, for there are militant murmurings amongst your contentious kith and kin. The slightest insensitive comment will spark off a belligerent blaze of wounding words and hostile actions, so if you want to avoid all-out warfare with your relatives you'll have to use every ounce of diplomacy and tact. Explosive astral energies indicate a difficult day.

TUESDAY, 28th. Some of your pals are a great deal more prosperous than you, but due to natural reticence and also a strong streak of false pride you're reluctant to admit it publicly. That's your business, but you'll find it is an attitude that could lead you into hot water financially if you try to live up to a luxurious lifestyle you can't possibly afford just to avoid losing face. Honesty is your best policy now, as any pals who drop you were not worth knowing anyway.

WEDNESDAY, 29th. Self-discipline and sticking to a rigid routine has never held the least appeal for you, and that's especially evident now as you play the part of free spirit for all it's worth. Don't take that as a criticism, for it is by being your own person, unbowed by the petty pressures of status and prestige, that you set such an inspiring example to folk with less courage and conviction. Inspired intuitive ideas flood your mind now.

THURSDAY, 30th. You're not keen to let the whole world in on the secret, but beneath your cool exterior you're fairly fizzing with excitement about a totally original idea, invention or concept you've dreamed up all on your own. Keep the wraps on your train of thought until you've ironed out all the wrinkles, for then you'll be in a prime position to take full credit for making a brilliant breakthrough possible. What a genius!

FRIDAY, 31st. If your love-life has been languishing in a listless lull for some time you can expect a few energetic improvements from today as the planet of physical passion and ardent affection takes up residence in your horoscopic house of romantic rapture and creative enthusiasm. An affair of the heart that begins now will bring a very agreeable air of excitement into your life, whilst solo Aquarians will soon feel the piercing pleasure of Cupid's amorous arrows. If romance just isn't your scene you should pour your excess energies into a creative or sporting venture.

SEPTEMBER

SATURDAY, 1st. If you have nippers of your own your personal resources of patience are probably beginning to run very low, so instead of dreading another weekend of whining and wheedling why not take your offspring out for a day's entertainment? You could try to tire them out with some energetic activities that'll at least guarantee a peaceful evening! If you're unencumbered by kids you have a splendid chance to live it up a little at a lively disco, dance or shindig.

SUNDAY, 2nd. One of the things you like about your other half is their unquestioning faith in your ability to tackle any task, however great, or even gargantuan! You're no shrinking violet, but even you must pause and assess your realistic chances of success at the latest extravagant idea they've come up with. You're deeply touched by their faith in your superhuman abilities, but don't let that lead you to bite off far more than you can chew!

MONDAY, 3rd. Love is the name of this Monday's galactical game, whether you're in a steady relationship of many years' standing or poised on the breathtaking brink of total togetherness. Whatever your marital and romantic status, there are people in your world who'll be thrilled to bits if you just show them a little extra affection and appreciation now. All it takes is a kindly word or perhaps a small gift and you'll earn undying adoration!

TUESDAY, 4th. There are some very silly rumours abroad on the subject of a personal problem of yours and if you weren't personally involved you'd just have to laugh out loud at the way some folk can twist the truth without even realising it. Have a quiet word in the ear of anyone else involved to mae sure they're not taken in by the garrulous gossips and you'll be able to stand back with an amused smile on your face. Don't over-react, for by keeping your head you'll easily defuse any dangerous implications.

WEDNESDAY, 5th. There's an unavoidable astral emphasis on your economic standing so don't pretend to yourself that all is well on the financial front when it is not. Fiscal strategies and monetary methods that served you well in the past just aren't appropriate to the extra economic pressures of the present-day world and it is up to you to bring your budgetary tactics up to date. Either discuss your situation with an accountant or your bank manager, or sink slowly but surely into debt.

THURSDAY, 6th. You're in for a thrilling Thursday if you throw yourself into the sociable spirit of the day, from packing in plenty of parties and gala gatherings to taking part in a sporting interest left over from your more active and energetic schooldays. A youngster has a few original ideas about ways and means of eliciting the maximum enjoyment from a given situation, so don't be too proud to join in the fun. You're a playful pussy cat these days!

FRIDAY, 7th. Luxury-loving Venus slips seductively into your eighth house of shared resources and erotic pleasure, ushering in a physically, emotionally and financially fantastic phase. Take time out from your restless roamings to sample the earthly delights of an intimate affair and at the same time talk to a bountiful benefactor who may bail you out of dire economic straits. Your personal portfolio of professional contacts should be put into action to help you overcome a challenge to your authority and expertise.

SATURDAY, 8th. You've been as busy as the proverbial bee all week and now you crave the contemplative company of your own inner thoughts without the incessant interruptions of less perceptive folk. Anyone who tries to engage you in inconsequential chit-chat will quickly give it up as a bad job as there's no way you're about to descend to trifling or trivial topics just now. You're a deep one this weekend, and that's just the way you like it!

SUNDAY, 9th. You can't help feeling you've done an admirable job of work on the family accounts, from settling an outstanding bill to arranging for more equitable treatment from the taxman. The trouble is you're so clever folk are beginning to take you for granted and may not have noticed the many miracles you've pulled off on their behalf! Publicise your superb successes a little more openly and you'll earn the appreciation you deserve.

MONDAY, 10th. You're very bright-eyed and bushy-tailed today, even if it is a mundane Monday. Could it have something to do with the fact that your love-life is beginning to take off in a most flattering and frolicsome manner? If that seems a forlorn hope just wait till you've met some of the sensationally seductive folk waiting to waylay you now, for you'll soon have a happy grin adorning your face!

TUESDAY, 11th. When it comes to a meeting of minds you and the love of your life are an enchanting example to us all for you each intuitively seem to know just what'll bring the other the maximum pleasure and gratification. On a purely material plane however it is a very different picture, as you both have some very set standards that don't exactly concur or correspond. Economic arguments will abound if you can't accept each other's alternatives.

WEDNESDAY, 12th. 'Out of the mouths of babes' goes the old saying, and today you'll have a chance to discover just how close to the bone an innocent remark uttered by a naïve youngster can be. They don't mean to upset or unnerve you, but whether it's your own children or a neighbouring nipper prattling playfully in your hearing, you can't help being deeply touched by their observations. You're not such a hard-boiled old Aquarian, are you?

THURSDAY, 13th. Your physical condition has been causing concern for some time, and even though your ailments may be relatively minor it's much better to be safe than sorry. Take yourself off to an expert for a thorough check-up for once you've been given the all-clear you'll sleep more easily. You may not have too much faith in conventional medical wisdom, so perhaps you'd be better off consulting someone skilled in the alternatives?

FRIDAY, 14th. You're such a conscientious and diligent soul you're apt to take on far more than your fair share of the responsibilities at work, but it's becoming clear to you that it's not fair on anyone, least of all yourself, to continue in this assiduous vein. Quietly stick to your principles and work to a more reasonable and equitable pace, for no one has cause for complaint. Give yourself a break!

SATURDAY, 15th. Anyone who thought you were totally indifferent to the appeal of amour should listen in to your private conversations today, for your 'ice-maiden or man' image will melt away in a matter of moments under such a torrent of tenderness! Set yourself the sweet challenge of winning the heart of someone you've fancied from afar and you'll soon realise you have not lost your romantic touch. A divine day for whispering words of adoration and affection in the ear of someone you love.

SUNDAY, 16th. This is really a most delicate and delicious day as the harmonious heavens help you begin to understand your emotional and sexual desires more. A purely platonic relationship may be just as fulfilling and rewarding as an affair that is openly amorous, as you're acutely aware of the pleasure to be gained from a love that operates on a spiritual level.

MONDAY, 17th. Keep your eyes wide open and your ears pricked up and alert on Monday and you'll pick up some absorbing clues to a monetary mystery that has aroused your interest recently. There's no need as yet to suspect foul play, but don't let that stop you from keeping your sleuthing skills sharpened up. You have a cunning combination of intelligence and intuition at your disposal and can see through the most elaborate excuse or explanation with ease.

TUESDAY, 18th. On the face of it you're up against a formidable opposition careerwise, from rivals who are after your position to authoritarian autocrats who dislike your refusal to kowtow to the status quo. But that's not the whole picture, for you've got quite a few friends in high places to your credit. When the chips are down you'll find the required resources are to hand to aid you in your ambitions, whether it's financial backing or moral support you seek.

WEDNESDAY, 19th. In the past you've often played fast and loose with the official rules and regulations in this country, but recent developments have made it abundantly clear to you that this is a very shaky basis for your more elevated ambitions. Turn over a new leaf with regard to your attitude to the secular and spiritual authorities and you'll find life very much easier and much more relaxing.

THURSDAY, 20th. In your heart you know you have what it takes to rise rapidly to the very top of your particular specialised field, whether it's professional prestige, social cachet or personal fulfilment you seek. A certain investment of cash, time and effort is required before you can live up to your full potential, but there are plenty of powerful backers and admiring fans to help you on your way. Don't let false pride prevent you from summoning support when it's needed. After all, knowing when to utilise aid and assistance is a sign of strength, not weakness!

FRIDAY, 21st. Restless rays drifting down from the fretful heavens make you wonder what you're missing in life as you follow the herd in the pursuit of success and standing. You're filled with a heartfelt hankering after adventure so take immediate steps to introduce a few radical changes into your daily programme. I wouldn't recommend making a total break with tradition just now, so assuage your thirst for excitement by making minor adjustments to your routine.

SATURDAY, 22nd. You just can't be pinned down to a single category these days, and anyone who tries will end up perplexed and puzzled by your many contradictions. As far as you're concerned it's no problem, for you do not see why you shouldn't turn your hand to pragmatic practicalities just as easily as you explore the abstract ideas involved in a spiritual, moral and ethical outlook. Dominating all your disparate and dissimilar activities, however, is an overriding concern with helping folk who are less fortunate than yourself.

SUNDAY, 23rd. A dazzling day dawns for the autumn Equinox points you down the positive and promising path of intellectual expansion and personal growth. You're soused in star-luck as you realise what a riveting range of possibilities lies open to your intrigued and excited mind. International inklings attract you as never before, so maybe a foreign trip or learning another language should be your next step? Push back all boundaries and prepare to roam free!

MONDAY, 24th. You have some pretty erudite and educated pals in your social circle, so why not pick their brains to help to settle an argument? You're such a culture-vulture these days you'll leap at any chance to discuss issues involving the arts, architecture or musical amenities of your area. Whilst you're at it maybe it would be worth joining a group or society dedicated to certain civilised principles?

TUESDAY, 25th. Is it something you said? You must have made a *faux pas* somewhere along the line lately, as every time you join a group of your normally cheerful chums an unnatural silence falls as if they're trying to keep something from you. It's a most upsetting mystery as you hate to feel you're out in the cold, but it may take tact and tenacity to get to the bottom of it. An emotionally tense and trying day.

WEDNESDAY, 26th. You have a pretty powerful, perceptive and penetrating mind at your disposal, so turn your cerebral spotlight on the problem of achieving your full professional and social potential. A timely tip from someone whose attainments you admire will point out a path to the top that's not obvious at first sight but on deeper reflection makes perfect sense. Devise a more subtle strategy for success and you'll go far!

THURSDAY, 27th. Your attention is irresistibly drawn inward by the perceptive planetary partnership of the Moon, Uranus and Neptune, urging you to investigate the many intuitive, psychic or supernatural ideas that lie beneath the surface of your mind. As far as the pure practicalities of life are concerned you're about as useful as an ice-cube in an igloo so don't plan to produce too much in the way of positive results just yet.

FRIDAY, 28th. After your day of delicious dreams and mysterious reveries you feel the need to restore the balance of your world by getting down to brass tacks and thinking out the purely practical outcome of the supernatural subjects you've been investigating. There may be the chance to make a certain amount of rich revenue from your artistic or intuitive skills if you set up a suitable support structure and put the marketing in reliable hands, so ponder the pragmatic potential now.

SATURDAY, 29th. So long as you expect the unexpected and don't mind adapting to ever-changing conditions you're in for an exciting and exhilarating day on this Saturday, for Uranus the rebel is activated by belligerent sunbeams. An unexpected visitor from afar or a journey to an area that's entirely new to you are just some of the stimulating and surprising possibilities in the stars for you. Don't cling to a rigid routine, for at the moment that's a forlorn hope.

SUNDAY, 30th. Now's your chance to make creative capital out of your unusual experiences this weekend as you're primed and ready to take a positive and artistically or socially enterprising view of all that's occurred. Aquarians with a taste for the arts should energetically follow up an influx of inspirations, whilst if you're more interested in being the life and soul of a gregarious gathering an off-the-cuff invitation will assemble an intriguing array of acquaintances.

OCTOBER

MONDAY, 1st. A late holiday or long-distance journey under-taken during the next few weeks is so superbly starred you're in for a tremendous treat, whether you're on the look-out for an exotic romance or simply seek a change of scene. You're also entering a period when artistic and cultural excellence is increasingly important to you, so take an educated lead from your sophisticated soul mate and immerse yourself in fine music, good books and other elevating subjects.

TUESDAY, 2nd. It's been a long, expensive summer, and there are outstanding bills and budgetary imbalances to be attended to before you launch yourself in the next phase of your year. You're imbued with all the common sense and prudent wisdom required to find out exactly where you're straying from the guidelines you've laid down for yourself. By assessing your economic state in detail now you'll quickly put a stop to any flaws and failings.

WEDNESDAY, 3rd. On a purely personal level you're filled with pecuniary prudence, but when it comes to responding to an emotional appeal from someone who's in trouble you're kindness personified. You prefer to hide your true sentimental reasons behind a rational and reasonable façade, but the fact is that you're a soft touch for anyone with a suitably sad and sorrowful sob-story.

THURSDAY, 4th. It's time you took a fresh look at some of the routines and systems governing your lifestyle, for in some ways you're not making the most of your full creative and intellectual capacity. This is a golden opportunity to talk openly with someone about a communications failure between you, for however reluctant you may be to uncover an emotional hang-up, only through admitting its existence do you stand a chance of putting it behind you. Prepare the path for a fresh beginning.

FRIDAY, 5th. You're brimming over with bright ideas and promising projects, but every positive possibility seems to be almost immediately foiled and frustrated by personal perplexities or paranoias which have little firm foundation in fact. Weigh up the pros and cons before you commit yourself to any major enterprise this Friday for you're mentally clouded and confused. In the weeks ahead you'll be in a much better position to sort out your ideals, principles and priorities.

SATURDAY, 6th. Your varied convictions and commitments may seem pretty straightforward to you, but take pity on people with a less nimble brain, for you've got a finger in so many pies some folk just can't make you out. For the most part that suits you fine, as you really prefer to keep the *hoi polloi* at a distance, but when it comes to communing with the people you admire and respect you will have to get your message across in a less muddled and manic way.

SUNDAY, 7th. On the face of it there's nothing much doing this Sunday, but there's no need to take that as a cue for curling up into a ball and simply switching off. Why not take the opportunity of a peaceful day of rest to attend to a few chores around the home? I know mowing the lawn, putting up shelves or doing the laundry really isn't the highlight of your week, but you'll find a surprising amount of satisfaction in putting your domestic world in apple-pie order.

MONDAY, 8th. Theoretically you've nothing at all against the mundane chores of life, but there's no denying that your spirits receive a lift at the prospect of a more interesting and stimulating day ahead of you. Contacts with people overseas will inject an extra air of excitement into your working world, whilst home-bound Aquarians should concentrate on enjoying a little extra social life. Youngsters bring a gleam of pure joy to your eyes now.

TUESDAY, 9th. Let's face it Aquarians, you're born rebels, and any opportunity that arises to cock a snook at authority is as irresistible to you as a brightly wrapped sweetie to a child! That's certainly obvious this Tuesday as you speak your mind about a revolutionary opinion you hold that's guaranteed to jolt less forward-looking folk wide awake. You derive a great deal of gleeful enjoyment from the outraged expression on some folk's faces, but in the long run you could suffer from the secret enemies you've made.

WEDNESDAY, 10th. If anyone asked for an off-the-cuff opinion you'd instantly come out in favour of the idea of enhancing your level of learning and education, but there are limits to the time and energy available even to a superhuman Water-Carrier! Don't bite off more than you can chew just to save face and keep up your culturally advanced image. Spend some time with a colleague who's coping with a crisis, for a sympathetic and understanding ear will work wonders.

THURSDAY, 11th. Everything seems to be going swimmingly this Thursday as you chat cheerfully with your chums and discuss a positive plan with your other half, but you're deluding yourself dangerously if you try to kid yourself that emotional consider-ations can be ignored. Watch out for someone who professes to have your best interests at heart but who proceeds to undermine you with sly hints and subtle innuendoes. Steer well clear of all financial transactions, for your judgment's not at its impartial best.

FRIDAY, 12th. You'll need to keep your wits about you today as well, for there's a very mixed and muddled astral array in the heavens. All you crave is plenty of personal freedom to do your own thing, which doesn't seem too much to ask, but there's something about the way you voice your desires that'll create some perverse and peculiar opposition to your ideas. Trying to make some folk understand what you're after is just like beating your head against a brick wall, so save your breath for a more open and auspicious day.

SATURDAY, 13th. Quick, whilst there's a clearing in the fog surrounding your world, put your ideas in writing or insist on an audience with someone you need to contact and you'll finally make your point with the punch and impact you'd hoped for. An unusually enlightened youngster will urge you to take up an interest in a more energetic way, and if I were you I'd heed their encouraging words.

SUNDAY, 14th. There's a fierce flame of passion burning deep within your heart, fuelling a fervently amorous fantasy that provides you with so much personal pleasure you see no reason to abandon your dream world for the boring banalities of harsh reality. There are spoilsports around who'll try to burst your bubble of delight, but part of the fun derives from your ability to keep less imaginative folk guessing. You're such a dark horse!

MONDAY, 15th. As irritable Martian rays rattle the easy-going equanimity of Mother Moon on this Monday you can expect a time of edgy, uptight and anxious contact with the people you meet. A child will prove particularly cantankerous and cranky, but before you mete out an on-the-spot punishment check to see that they're not simply overtired. Steer clear of controversy on this argumentative day.

TUESDAY, 16th. Everything's going so well these days as every project you propose meets with a positive response and your dearest desires appear to be on the point of coming true, so why do you feel so blue? There is nothing in your external circumstances to account for your despondent and despairing mood, so instead you should look within for psychologically based fears and purely emotional anxieties. It'll help to understand the source of your worries for then you can get set to shake them off.

WEDNESDAY, 17th. If you're on the look-out for a suitably seductive, stimulating and sensational soul mate you may be disappointed if you restrict your range to your immediate neighbourhood, for your current amorous stars favour a much more adventuresome outlook. Anything from an overseas friend to a potential romance with someone from a different cultural background should be considered, for even if you're happily married you'll relish the friendship of folk from afar.

THURSDAY, 18th. Think over your own cultural background and dogmatic assumptions this Thursday, for there's a New Moon calling to you and pointing the way to a brand new opening in your life. Forget out-dated fascinations and launch yourself into a subject that's more in keeping with this modern world, as only by keeping pace with the influx of new information and novel ideas can you claim to be a child of your times.

FRIDAY, 19th. Your claim to be completely impartial and objective is given the lie this Friday, for when it comes to a little furtive flattery from your other half you're as likely as anyone to overestimate your own abilities and aptitudes! I know your potential for doing good in this world is exceptional and extraordinary, but you'll quickly lose the common touch if you allow an inflated ego to take control of your actions. A little more modesty wouldn't go amiss!

SATURDAY, 20th. Delve deeply into your inner self and you'll discover a powerful streak of immovable ambition to make your mark in the world as someone to be taken seriously. However much you try to kid yourself that it's enough simply to keep your head above water, you will never be truly satisfied with yourself until you've achieved something of note. Whether it is in terms of a career or through doing your bit to improve the ways of society you're determined to make an impact.

SUNDAY, 21st. As you continue to contemplate your imposing ambitions and wonder about the best way to seize the initiative you can't help feeling a trifle daunted at the stupendous size of the task you've set yourself. No one could accuse you of lacking courage or commitment, but maybe you should consider a less demanding role for yourself? There's really no point in driving yourself into an early grave just for the sake of satisfying your ego!

MONDAY, 22nd. If you have relatives overseas or friends who are far away you should seize the opportunity this Monday to get in touch, whether it is via the phone, a letter, or a messenger, for who knows when you'll next get round to making the effort? Mentally you're on the ball today, able to sort out the most complex and confusing items of information with ease, so don't waste too much time on trivialities.

TUESDAY, 23rd. Both the Sun and Mercury slide secretively into Scorpio today and as far as you're concerned it has set the cat amongst your professional pigeons. There are envious folk around in your career world who will resent the obvious ambition gleaming in your eyes, but before you take up an entrenched position you must try to talk things through. Rivals, competitors and adversaries prove much more amenable to the powerful voice of reason than you expect.

WEDNESDAY, 24th. From the mischievous grin on your face I'm forced to conclude that there's an ace up your sleeve that will totally transform your position with regard to a cause that to all intents and purposes appears to be lost. You're not about to reveal your full hand, for you love to string people along and keep them wondering. You're such a tease!

THURSDAY, 25th. Venus reaches a position of prominence in your solar chart this Thursday as she steps into Scorpio and instantly endows you with the diplomatic skills required to win the whole-hearted support and admiring applause of the powers

126

that be. A female boss may prove particularly understanding and helpful, but only if you have the wit and good taste to avoid making an outright threat on her own professional position. This is a productive period for all promotion prospects.

FRIDAY, 26th. Anyone who thought they'd got you and your ambitions taped will be forced to eat their words today, for you're way ahead of them and are busy devising a totally new plan of action. It may be worth considering an entirely different career if you're beginning to get bored with your present post, or maybe a demand for more flexible working conditions will be enough to keep you interested? A fascination with modern technology will bear fertile fruit in terms of your career.

SATURDAY, 27th. Your other half is coming up with some astonishing ideas these days as they cast off all inhibitions and decide to live life to the full, come what may! You're thrilled by such an enthusiastic and optimistic attitude, but you can't help wondering if they're not going a bit too far out on a limb. You hate to counsel caution and dampen their spirits, but someone's got to keep their feet on the ground!

SUNDAY, 28th. Luscious lunar rays illuminate your very own sign on Sunday, and as a result you're awash with emotion and sensitive sentiment. Memories of your youth come back to you, triggered by anything from a half-forgotten tune to an old snapshot you encounter. You're not normally keen on wasting time on a maudlin wander down memory lane, but it wouldn't hurt to make an exception for once. After all, there are so many happy times to be recalled. A highly emotive day.

MONDAY, 29th. Even if you're an affluent Aquarian you're not immune from money worries, for like most of us you need to know you're making the most of your economic assets. In fact, if you check over the latest figures from your bank or accountant you'll have good reason to feel quietly content, for you're managing really rather well considering the difficulties. A raise may be in the offing that'll ease the pecuniary pressures even more.

TUESDAY, 30th. An unexpected encounter whilst you're doing your daily rounds today will offer a golden opportunity on a silver platter for you to step up a few rungs on the ladder of worldly success and status. It may be an old flame who's now attained a position of power or an entirely new contact who is charmed by your unconventional outlook. Don't let false modesty or reticent reserve keep you from using your personal charms to gain an advantage!

WEDNESDAY, 31st. A surprise communication that appears on your doormat or via a chance encounter may induce an acute attack of anxiety for at first sight it seems your emotional and material security could be threatened by some unexpected developments. Before you go off the deep end you really must make sure you have all the facts as some people have a very weird sense of humour and you could be the butt of an incompetent and unkind practical joke.

NOVEMBER

THURSDAY, 1st. My advice to you, my friends, on this thrilling Thursday is to put on your prettiest frock or smartest suit and sally forth to make your fortune in the world, for there aren't many people who could resist your dazzling combination of sheer charm, charisma and appeal. It's a fantastic day for an interview or appointment with people in power, for you'll have them eating out of your hand once you unleash your full allure on them! Strike whilst the iron is hot and ask for a hefty raise, for they'll hate to turn you down.

FRIDAY, 2nd. Friday's blast of Moonpower gives you fair warning that a family feud or distracting domestic dilemma must be resolved once and for all. Don't let stupid sentiment stop you from ridding yourself of old or shabby possessions that are cluttering up your home. On the careers front you should insist on a meeting with someone at the very top, for you have some far-reaching ideas that could transform your profession and place you in a much more prominent position.

SATURDAY, 3rd. Guilt, jealousy, possessiveness . . . it's not a particularly edifying list of emotions, but that's the flavour of your feelings this weekend. It is someone in your family who has stirred up this sensitive storm of overwrought passions, so rather than taking it out on all and sundry, use it as an opportunity to settle an old score and let some light into a subject you've been suppressing for far too long. It's better out than in!

SUNDAY, 4th. Quadruple contacts criss-cross the heavens this Sunday and spotlight your worldly ambitions from almost every angle you can think of. There's no escaping the conclusion that you must think through your aims and aspirations in depth, ensuring that they truly represent your spiritual values and the expectations of your loved ones as well as satisfying your natural desire for egotistical advancement. It's a tall order, but you have the wit, wisdom and far-sighted acumen required.

MONDAY, 5th. There are some fantastic parties planned for tonight's celebrations, but by the time evening comes you could be feeling like a battered version of old Guy Fawkes as you're torn between the conflicting demands and desires of your partner in life as against the bosses of this world. You're gallantly trying to keep everyone happy, and the only loser will be you if you don't keep sight of your own ideals and aspirations.

TUESDAY, 6th. You really are your own worst enemy sometimes aren't you? With the very best of intentions you set out to strike a blow on behalf of the underprivileged and unfortunate of this world, but somehow your generous gesture is misconstrued as an all-out attack on the very people you're trying to help. It's a classic conundrum, and rather than get yourself any deeper in the soup maybe you should lie low for a wee while until you can see a more effective way to act. Nervous tension mounts, so try to relax.

WEDNESDAY, 7th. If you didn't manage to calm down yesterday you'll be paying the price now in terms of vanished vitality and ailing health. It's high time you treated yourself with much more care and consideration, so cancel any tasks that'll take too much out of you and instead arrange for a total respite from pressures of every kind. Once you've had a good rest you'll soon be back to your usual ebullient self.

THURSDAY, 8th. You're engaged in a battle of wills with an authoritarian autocrat this Thursday over an intractable issue concerning your prestige and position, and things will come bubbling to the boil if neither of you backs down pretty smartish. Your ultimate audacious aim is to utterly defeat any power-mad people who foolishly try to confront, confine or constrict you. You're a formidable force these days, but by giving in to an unworthy taste for revenge and retaliation you'll store up trouble for yourself in the future.

FRIDAY, 9th. Time for a little light relief, I should think, the heavens are in agreement as they lift your spirits and instil a marvellous mood of good-humoured happiness to help make this a fun-filled Friday. Why not take a day away from your duties and whisk your other half off for a complete change of scene? It'll do you both the world of good to take your attention entirely off the petty problems and trivial troubles that have filled your week. Pack up your troubles in an old kit-bag!

SATURDAY, 10th. Saturday sees a planetary time-bomb set off in your solar house of ego and ambitions as the Sun and Pluto form their potent powers into a single driving force. Total transformation careerwise has become the unavoidable conclusion, so why try to fight against the inevitable? If you're completely at a loss talk it over with a kindly colleague, for they'll speak sound sense and help you to put your own thoughts in order.

SUNDAY, 11th. Volatile Mercurial vibes give a very welcome boost to your flagging social life from Sunday, reminding you of the inexhaustible supplies of goodwill and affection available amongst your faithful friends. Don't rely totally on acquaintances who derive solely from your past, as this is an excellent opportunity to forge some new links and expand the circumference of your social circle. Friendship forms the focus of your world in the weeks ahead, so don't stand alone.

MONDAY, 12th. You're known as an intuitive expert, but inspiration and insight on their own aren't enough to provide the guidance you need. Fortunately you're also blessed with a sound streak of common sense, and when you combine the two, as you do today, you're virtually unbeatable. Use your superb skills to work out a more effective and efficient way to help the needy, as you hate to feel your clever words and ideas have no practical application.

TUESDAY, 13th. You've put in some sterling work on a charitable appeal recently, helping with the organisation from behind the scenes and generously giving your time and effort with no thought of reward. That's precisely the kindly quality that will earn for you an acknowledgement from someone you respect and admire today, and that means more to you than the most extravagant praise from lesser folk. Maybe you should think of making a career out of a compassionate interest?

WEDNESDAY, 14th. They say that pride comes before a fall, and that seems to be your predicament today. Some people with no understanding of all you've achieved against the odds may cast unkind aspersions that wound you deeply. Actually the tittle-tattle of uninformed folk really shouldn't concern you, for the people who really matter won't be taken in by their malicious gossip. Your false fears will soon vanish.

THURSDAY, 15th. What did I tell you? The worries that were weighing on you so much yesterday lift from your shoulders as if they had never existed, leaving you with a fresh, hopeful and optimistic outlook on life. An official who has always taken a hard line with you in the past should be approached with an entirely different attitude and viewpoint, for you will be astonished to discover how much your own unspoken opinions affect the way others react to you. Maybe those uncompromising autocrats aren't such bad sticks after all!

FRIDAY, 16th. I know you're fearfully busy this Friday, what with one thing and another, but you should take just a little time to think deeply about where your life is leading. Is your current career living up to your hopes and expectations? Are your present relations with the powers that be gradually heading for heartbreak? By making minor adjustment to your emotional attitude and outlook now you can avoid many complex problems in the future. Dig deep within . . . what do you really want to achieve?

131

SATURDAY, 17th. The astral emphasis now is clearly on your career concerns as the piercing light of the New Moon brings a forceful focus to bear, insisting on a brand new professional beginning of some sort. It's a superb time to lay the foundations of a much more ambitious era of personal achievement. Don't let an envious friend put you off your stroke with their cutting and caustic comments.

SUNDAY, 18th. Splendidly sociable stars launch you into an amiable, amicable and affable era this weekend as lusciously loving Venus fills your solar house of friendships with her romantic radiance. Prepare to enjoy the fabulous fruits of your personal popularity! A female friend who makes your acquaintance in the coming weeks will help teach you a thing or two about enjoying yourself to the full.

MONDAY, 19th. Roll out the red carpet, hang out a bit of bunting and generally set yourself up for a day of celebration, for generous Jupiterian vibes mingle with Mercury's eloquently expressive influence. Whoever you speak to today is sure to give a very positive response to any ideas you care to put forward, whether you're urging your other half to up sticks and emigrate or want to persuade a prosperous pal to back a pet project. An optimistic outlook is thoroughly justified now.

TUESDAY, 20th. Anyone who thought they had finally got you figured out will have to admit the error today for you don't even know what you'll be thinking and feeling yourself from one minute to the next, so how can anyone else be expected to keep pace? A hunch about a fraught family situation appears to be the solution you've been seeking, but you should not count your chickens until you've applied the test of time.

WEDNESDAY, 21st. Your attention is irresistibly drawn inward on this wistful Wednesday for the magical Moon is enmeshed in a nebulous net of Neptune's making. It's a fine time to investigate the intuitive, psychic or supernatural ideas and insights that lie beneath the surface of your mind. Where practicalities are concerned you are far from being at your best, as you're fully occupied with your visionary inner world.

THURSDAY, 22nd. You're entering a time of positive promise now the glorious golden rays of the Sun move into Sagittarius and illuminate your house of hopes and wishes. Waste no time in getting in touch with people who mean a lot to you, and whilst you're at it why not chivvy up your social life? In addition to enjoying the congenial company of agreeable acquaintances in the coming weeks you should concentrate on a cause that's crucial to your future objectives.

FRIDAY, 23rd. If you've made the mistake of taking a ravishing romantic partner for granted you'll rue your error this Friday as they show an independent spirit and decide to take matters into their own hands. Come to that, you're a trifle fed up with being taken for a sucker yourself and want to show beyond a shadow of doubt that you're nobody's fool. It's all very dramatic, but wouldn't it be better to talk things through and adopt a few concessions on either side? The course of true love is running very rough just now!

SATURDAY, 24th. You're automatically inclined to play the revolutionary rebel when folk around you reveal a despotic and dictatorial streak, and that's the position this weekend. Your immediate response to a tyrannical order someone has issued is instantly to take up the opposite position, but why not try a more compromising course of action? You'll have the satisfaction of seeing the surprise on the face of your intended adversary as they realise the fight's off!

SUNDAY, 25th. Your unconventional and unorthodox friends show a fine disregard for the trivial topic of mere material and monetary security, as their heads are so wrapped up in idealistic clouds they've completely forgotten the facts of life. Some people seem to think there's a certain spiritual superiority to be gained from disowning an interest in economics, but in your heart of hearts you know full well that you have a normal desire for money and possessions, and I for one don't see anything against it. Don't let moral blackmail get to you.

MONDAY, 26th. As if to reinforce my comments today's sky heralds a highly practical, pragmatic and productive day when

133

your personal possessions and finances can be repaired, restored and reorganised to make the most of your assets. A rumour that's been going round on the grapevine concerning an organisation you're connected with may be more than just hearsay.

TUESDAY, 27th. Mighty Mars is up to his turbulent tricks once more, but this time the all-powerful Sun is standing by to issue an astral challenge. The consequent combat concerns your creative concerns and pet projects, for you're up against some friends who feel you've poached on their personal preserve. You're not about to take an arrogant claim like that lying down, but an all-out argument is unlikely to resolve anything. It may be most enjoyable, but only through compromise on both sides will you restore the peace.

WEDNESDAY, 28th. You delight in making unconventional pronouncements designed to shock and surprise the people around you, but every so often your jokes and japes can misfire and cause genuine upset to someone who's much more sensitive than you supposed. There's a fine line between being outspoken and being objectionable, and you're skating very close to it this Wednesday. Put your brain into gear before you open your motormouth!

THURSDAY, 29th. The blessings of heaven rain down on you in a sumptuous and splendid shower, for whatever you do now you can hardly put a foot wrong! All one-to-one affairs are soused in sensational star-luck, whether you're long married or about to meet the soul mate of your dreams. This is a fantastic day for all social outings and excursions, from a merry meeting at your local to a far-flung holiday on foreign shores.

FRIDAY, 30th. This is a go-ahead period for all partnerships in your life, make no mistake, but the source of your present good fortune, jocular Jupiter, has decided to take a wee detour and in the process will put some of your more ambitious mutual ideas on ice. You'll need to adjust your timetable to take into account the fact that openings and opportunities will take a little extra effort to pursue, but in the long run this is just a very minor hold-up in your hopes.

DECEMBER

SATURDAY, 1st. Everyone you bump into on your routine rounds today seems to have a kind word and a message of encouragement for you and before long you'll have the overwhelming impression that the entire neighbourhood is behind you in a project you've taken on recently. It's a wonderfully warm feeling, but at the same time you can't help wondering if all this bonhomie and backslapping means you've taken on rather more than you bargained for. You're a trifle tense.

SUNDAY, 2nd. Mini Mercury's rational rays are dimmed and distorted as he wanders wistfully into your solar house of visions and fantasies, auguring a super-sensitive span when you're mentally attuned to your subconscious intuition, but totally out of touch with the down-to-earth facts of life. Don't let your distracted mood make you overlook a behavioural problem in a youngster close to you, as it's time you thrashed things out once and for all.

MONDAY, 3rd. Your self-control is slipping, for even though you know there are some confidences you shouldn't betray anyone with an ounce of determination this Monday will have you blabbing about every secret you've ever heard. You don't mean to squeal on the people who trusted you, but you're such a chatterbox now you'll rattle on without realising what you're saying. Your best policy is to keep silent!

TUESDAY, 4th. You're a real sociable starlet normally, but there's a physical price to be paid for your popularity, and this seems to be the day of reckoning. I don't care how many entertaining invites are pencilled in in your diary, you'll just have to get some rest if you're to restore your batteries for the festive season ahead. Look after yourself Aquarius, for no one else will!

WEDNESDAY, 5th. It doesn't take long for you to get back on your feet, for you're fighting fit and raring to go already! There's an enchanting aura of amour in the air, so take a moment to meditate on your good fortune in having such a fantastic partner. If you've yet to meet your soul mate, you should mix and mingle with as many people as possible, for the chances are you're about to be bowled over by a red-hot romance!

THURSDAY, 6th. As far as I can see there are still stars in your eyes as you go about with a gargantuan grin on your face, clutching a marvellous memento of yesterday's romantic rendezvous. It's obvious that your future good fortune lies along the path of partnership, so forget all about making it on your own and instead set out to develop a winning team. Anything from a marriage made in heaven to a business association of unlimited potential is yours for the taking.

FRIDAY, 7th. This really has been one of the most wonderful weeks on record, and there's no need for you to decide the show is over yet, for your Friday stars are just as lusciously loving as ever. Even if romance is low on your list of personal priorities I've yet to meet an Aquarian who wasn't attached to the ideal of friendship, so set about attracting some positive and pleasing pals to your own social circle. Who could resist your sweet smile and appealing attitude?

SATURDAY, 8th. There are some fears, doubts and worries that are so sensitive and sore you have difficulty even putting them into words, although you're yearning for a little advice and encouragement. Take the problem to someone you know you can trust not to mock your misgivings, for they're far more intuitive than you suppose and will help you express your anxieties. They'll also have some sage and sensible advice to offer.

SUNDAY, 9th. A sexual relationship that's been a source of joy in the past appears to be heading for the rocks of jealousy and mistrust and there's nothing a cool Water-Carrier hates more! Your immediate impulse is to run a mile from a passionate partner who's becoming possessive, but are you sure that's fair? Don't leave a lover in the lurch because of a little emotional insecurity – by reassuring them you'll restore the delightful intimate ambience of your affair.

MONDAY, 10th. Jumping Jehosephat! That's your astonished and exhilarated response to a truly brilliant brainwave that knocks you for six this Monday. You can't explain where your ideas are coming from, but they're flowing thick and fast, and they're all of world-class calibre. My only concern is that you'll be so busy dreaming up ever more original, inventive and outrageously novel notions that you'll forget a good half of your insights. Maybe you should have someone follow you round with a notebook. You're an incredibly inspired Aquarian now.

TUESDAY, 11th. Festive fever seems to be taking over everyone you meet these days and to be honest you're finding it all terribly tedious. You've no objection to Yuletide celebrations, but shy away from the more commercialised aspects. If you're a wealthy Water-Carrier a wee trip to sunnier climes or the ski-slopes will soon restore your sense of humour. For most of us the monotony can be relieved by instigating a free-ranging discussion with some perceptive pals on the true meaning of the season.

WEDNESDAY, 12th. A piece of fine music perfectly performed, a lovely face glimpsed from afar or a sumptuous scent wafting by on the breeze all set your heart aflame from this Wednesday as Venusian vibes accentuate your taste for all that's refined in life. Indulge your more suave and sophisticated desires to the full during the coming weeks and you'll be in seventh heaven. Don't let a natural distaste for anything coarse or vulgar blind you to the practical realities of life though.

THURSDAY, 13th. There's much more to you than meets the eye, as anyone trying to take advantage of your apparent indifference to fame and fortune will find to their cost this Thursday. You like to promote a lackadaisical public image, but that doesn't mean you'll let less skilful folk pip you to the post professionally. In fact you have quite a few very effective tricks up your sleeve, and this might be the time to put them into action on your own behalf.

FRIDAY, 14th. Domestically speaking you'll be wondering what's hit you from Friday, for all-conquering Mars races into your solar house of the home. With Christmas almost upon us it's clear you'll have to take your frantic family in hand and organise a more effective campaign if your arrangements are to be made in time.

Why they must leave everything to the last minute is beyond you, but with drive and determination you can make sure everything's made ready for the festivities.

SATURDAY, 15th. To you it is perfectly plain that someone has to take charge of your family if you want to avoid a total fiasco this *Noël*, but you can hardly blame people for taking offence at your heavy-handed way of ordering them about. It may drive you to distraction when there's so much to do and so little time, but a little more patience and politeness is the only solution to the strained and stressful atmosphere. Calm down and take things one at a time!

SUNDAY, 16th. Sit back and survey the results of your all-out attack on your abode and then give yourself a good pat on the back, for you've earned it! In fact everyone agrees that you deserve a total break from domestic duties so take yourself off for an entertaining day out. Maybe there are friends you've been too busy to visit or a neighbour who'd welcome a chance to chat? Get out and about and take pleasure in your widespread popularity.

MONDAY, 17th. If you're faced with a no-win situation in your social circle this Monday you must seriously consider the possibility that a particular partnership has run its course and come to the end of the line. There's a positive plethora of promising new social openings and opportunities available to you so look on the bright side and realise that you'll have so much more time now to make new friends and pursue a more contemporary cause.

TUESDAY, 18th. Sleepy wee Mercury is jolted into wide-awake alertness once more by a blast of pure energy from unpredictable Uranus. Your intuition is as acute and perceptive as it's ever been, allowing you to see instantly through any lies or fibs folk try to pass off on you. You're seized by a sudden fascination with a supernatural or spiritual subject that could lead you along an unorthodox path in the pursuit of truth. You're a little bewildered, but very excited!

WEDNESDAY, 19th. Velvet Venus joins the controversial crowd of planets in your solar house of secrets and the unconscious on Wednesday and sets a few anxious alarm bells ringing on the subject of amour. You may be on the brink of bliss in a brand new relationship or about to put your present partnership on an entirely new footing. The reasons for your romantic restlessness aren't at all clear to you, so perhaps it would be wiser to think things through more thoroughly before you upset the love of your life for no good reason.

THURSDAY, 20th. You've been immersed in your own dream world for quite long enough, and it's time you took your place in the fantastic round of parties, revels and festivals. Dust off your glad rags and step out in style for the eyes of the world are upon you and this is your big chance to shine like the sensational superstar you are! If you've been feeling a bit flat about the festivities, spend some time with an excited child; they'll soon remind you of the magic of Christmas!

FRIDAY, 21st. Time is running very short, so are you quite sure you've bought a gift for your other half that truly reflects the depth of your appreciation for all they mean to you? When you reflect on the potential pleasure, passion and progress proffered by a future in their enthusiastic company you'll want to rush out and purchase a prezzie of spectacular proportions. Don't make the mistake of simply throwing cash at the problem, as a little careful thought will mean so much more than a mammoth price-tag.

SATURDAY, 22nd. This is the time of the year when you're instinctively inclined to retreat from life's rough-and-tumble and recharge your batteries in readiness for the days of jubilation and celebration that lie ahead. Delve fearlessly into the visionary vistas of your inner world and you'll uncover unsuspected resources of intuition to aid you in your spiritual search.

SUNDAY, 23rd. An utterly impossible but totally lovely dream of perfection has you totally entranced this Sunday as you intuitively understand the spiritually significant beauty of this loving festival. Don't be too disappointed if less sensitive folk seem oblivious to the aura of inspirations surrounding you, for it's not given to us all to understand these things. If you put your partner on a pedestal you'll only set them up for a fall, so be prepared for a few human failing in your loved ones.

MONDAY, 24th. You're really not of this world these days are you? If you're of a religious turn of mind you'll be in your element on your knees in a church or other place of prayer, for you're in tune with the divinely loving meaning of this season of goodwill. Maybe you prefer to express your ideals through helping folk less fortunate than yourself? Your compassionate and considerate aid will be deeply appreciated by everyone you meet now.

TUESDAY, 25th. You've been in a bit of a romantic reverie lately, but you're wide awake today, ready to throw yourself whole-heartedly into the fabulous fun that's lined up. You're deeply touched by your family's gifts and goodwill, but why restrict your celebrations to your immediate relatives? There are faithful friends and agreeable acquaintances to be included in your revelry so do the rounds of anyone within reach and you'll be in your convivial element!

WEDNESDAY, 26th. I do believe you've managed to talk yourself to a standstill! It may be a voice that's literally worn out or just a general feeling of lassitude and languor, but either way we'll be lucky to get a peep out of you today! Actually everyone else is just as subdued and sluggish, so why not gather round the home fire with your family and indulge in a day of total tranquillity? It's bliss!

THURSDAY, 27th. As you gradually surface from the sensationally satisfying surfeit of good food, good wine and wonderful company, you can't help turning your mind towards the prospect of your future professional plans. You have a useful lull in which to lick your strategy into shape, so assess your chances and aim for the heights! There are people who owe you a favour or two who ought to be included in your tactics, as they can be counted on to come up trumps.

FRIDAY, 28th. This first year of the new decade wouldn't be complete without a little time spent retracing your steps and appraising your progress on all fronts, whether you're mainly interested in career relationships or a pet pastime. It's far from being a futile operation, however reluctant you may be to face up to some of the failures as well as the many successes, for you'll only learn through experience. This is a perfect opportunity to look back briefly.

SATURDAY, 29th. It's party time all over again! I know it's not quite the New Year but I'm certain you and your pals can think of a suitable excuse to get out your glad rags and live it up a bit. You're at your good-humoured and gregarious best this Saturday so whatever you do don't deprive your friends of your cordial company. Let the good times roll!

SUNDAY, 30th. The positive and practical conclusions you made on the strength of your annum's experiences on Friday represent the better face of nostalgia, whereas under this Sunday's super-sensitive sky you're apt to indulge in the unproductive emotional indulgence of a purely sentimental stroll down memory lane. Don't let negative and fearful feelings take a hold, for they're not based on anything solid or substantial.

MONDAY, 31st. This very first year of the brand new decade is going out in sensational style, showered in scintillating star-luck from both the cataclysmic conjunction between the Sun and Uranus and also the fulminating Full Moon. It's time for a total turn around in the way you look after your physical, mental and emotional well-being, for with a radical rethink and some revolutionary resolutions you could become the Body Beautiful of 1991!

A Star Book
Published in 1989
by the Paperback Division of
W. H. Allen & Co Plc
Sekforde House, 175/9 St John Street
London, EC1V 4LL

Copyright © 1989 by Russell Grant

Phototypeset by Input Typesetting Ltd, London
Printed in Great Britain by
Cox & Wyman Ltd, Reading

Illustrations by Maggie Keen

ISBN 0 352 32514 3

This book is dedicated to Jacque Evans, my friend and guide.

Acknowledgements:
Many thanks to my right-hand lass, Wendy Fey, and also many
thanks to Jane Struthers.